The Burden of God

The Burden of God

Studies in wisdom and civilization from the book of Ecclesiastes

Michael W. Kelley

Contra Mundum Books
Minneapolis

Scripture quotations are from the Holy Bible, New
International Version. © 1973, 1978, 1984 International
Bible Society. Used by permission of Zondervan Bible
Publishers.

Published by Contra Mundum Books
PO Box 32652, Fridley MN 55432-0652

Set in Monotype Baskerville, 11.5 points
Manufactured in the United States of America

ISBN 0-9637768-0-0

For Kaylene

Ecclesiastes 9:9

Contents

Introduction

Ecclesiastes is a strangely fascinating book. Its seemingly inexhaustible supply of quoted and quotable "sayings" or aphorisms captivates minds for whom moralistic platitudes provide the only certainties. The book's stock phrases crop up everywhere among a diversity of authors, in various literary contexts, and for sundry purposes. One encounters references to them in works of history, psychology, philosophy, social theory, and novels, to mention but a few. In short, the quaint sayings of the book of Ecclesiastes are broadly familiar to our modern cultured elites and various *litterateurs,* and are not the sole preserve of theologians and Bible scholars, or even of writers of exclusively ethical concerns. Their terse formulaic expressions can easily lend themselves to proverbial dicta and moralizing axioms. Where they are not reproduced verbatim, they often appear to convey, in approximate words, the gist of what it is they are thought to mean. How familiar they are! And how readily they come to mind!—"Vanity of vanities, all is vanity," "There is nothing new under the sun," "For with much wisdom comes much sorrow; the more knowledge, the more grief," "There is a time for everything, and a season for every activity under heaven," "Man's fate is like that of the animals; the same fate awaits them both," "A cord of three strands is not quickly broken," "All man's efforts are for his mouth, yet his appetite is never satisfied," "As goods increase, so do those who consume them," "Cast your bread upon the waters, for

after many days you will find it again," "Remember your
Creator in the days of your youth," "Of the making of many
books there is no end, and much study wearies the body"—
the list seems endless. Yet, in spite of our acquaintance with
the clever aphorisms of Ecclesiastes, the book as a whole
remains an incomprehensible mystery—one huge conun-
drum smack in the middle of Holy Scripture! At its worst, it
is the strident morbidity of a bitterly negative and pessimistic man—a man for whom assuredly "the day of death [is]
better than the day of birth." (7:1)

For many Christians this seeming negativism of the book
of Ecclesiastes is especially troubling. As a result, like the
purveyors of modern moralism in general, when they cease
to moralize from the book—not knowing what to make of it
otherwise—they usually avoid it altogether. The explanation for this state of affairs is not far to seek. It stems from
the preconception which many Christians have of what the
"gospel" message contains, and in their minds the book of
Ecclesiastes does not convey that same message. At best,
Ecclesiastes is a preparation for the gospel's "good news,"
but not itself a bearer of that message. The problem, however, goes much deeper than this, for the concept of the gospel in many people's minds seems a very humanistic one. Its
lofty content has become man-centered and subjectivist-
experientialist in nature. Mawkish fashions of love and good
feelings have come to substitute for the redoubtable substance of the Christian faith. The chief concern is with man
and his needs rather than with God and His will. And when
we speak of man's needs we really mean man's "wants."
With this characteristic attitude we hardly hesitate to
demand that Scripture meet with our satisfaction above all
else. Once we view our personal experience as paramount,
the "gospel" content is bound to become nothing more than
a means to gratify that experience. It does not matter that it
may even be viewed as the "highest" means, it is exclusively
its "usefulness" for our experience that truly counts.

When our experience is measured by our perceptions,

and not by what God tells us it should be, it stipulates how we come to the Scripture as a whole. We unavoidably place conditions on what we think it must say. Christians have come to insist that God's Word should be immediately "practical," i.e., a suitable elixir for nourishing self esteem, a tonic for emotional tedium and feelings of boredom and alienation, a felicitous narcotic for the vexations of modern mass existence. To be sure, God's Word does have doctrine too. That is important up to a point, but one should not make too much of it. Besides, doctrine is so controversial. No two people, it seems, can agree on every detail of doctrine. Concern for truth is intellectualist and prideful. Of what good is it then? It serves no useful purpose. Is it not better to concentrate all our attention on those "practical" matters that are a common feature of every person's experience these days? Perhaps, this might not seem as objectionable as it would be if we permitted the Bible to tell us what it is that is practical for men to do. But in our narcissistic culture we have our own ideas, and Scripture had better conform to *our* idea of what is practical. Thus, if we cannot immediately discern the practicality of a portion of Scripture it is either passed over in silence or interpreted so as to please our prior sense of what is useful. Perhaps no book of Scripture has been so treated more than Ecclesiastes.

Ecclesiastes says nothing about "God's love." It is silent about His compassion and sympathy for hurting and ailing human beings. It lacks every indulgence of our present-day maudlin self-preoccupation. Instead of being warm, uplifting and positive, its message is cold, harsh and negative. How could something that is so insensitive to our predefined emotional and psychological needs possibly have anything useful to say? Not surprisingly, while Christians may accord it a place in their Bibles, they scarcely find room for it in their hearts and minds. For most, it remains a closed book.

The problem in understanding Ecclesiastes and discerning its importance in Scripture is deep-seated and pervasive.

It stems from the more general failure to understand God's Word as a whole, that it communicates a comprehensive message to man in the totality of his creation experience and existence in the world. Yet, while the Bible speaks to man, its content is principally about God to whom man must finally give account. The Bible provides the explanation for man's existence, it interprets the whole of life. It says that man was created to serve and to glorify God and to enjoy God forever. That is man's purpose; that is what his life is all about. All that he is and does should be rooted in and spring from that purpose. God meant that man in every aspect of his being should work out the implications of this, his chief reason for being.

The Bible is God's covenant word to man, over whom He claims exclusive sovereignty and authority. It tells of man's rebellion against God, and how as a result man's life has been cursed; that suffering and death are the penalty which he has justly merited for his disobedience. Despite this, and because God's judgement has been delayed, man proceeds confidently to erect his culture and civilization in an attitude of hostility toward God and with contempt for God's original purpose for man. Instead of building the Kingdom of God for the glory of God, man now seeks to build the kingdom of man to the glory of man. It is a sad and profound delusion, for God's curse on his life will frustrate every attempt on rebellious man's part to achieve anything of true worth. It is futile to strive against God. Still, man stubbornly and foolishly persists in his sinful rebellion. He is blind to the impossibility that his rebellion can succeed. This foolishness and stupidity of man is the great burden of the "wisdom literature" of Scripture, most especially of Ecclesiastes. One of the chief concerns of this "wisdom literature," and certainly of Ecclesiastes, is to disabuse sinful man of every possibility that his life can be fruitful of anything of lasting import—hence, the repeated assertion of the book that "all is vanity and chasing after wind." Apart from God that is all this life can be.

In order successfully to destroy man's belief in himself and his endeavors *apart from God*, the "wisdom literature"— Ecclesiastes in particular—proffers a powerfully negative message. Why this is so can perhaps be understood from a comment by C. Van Til: "in this world of sin no Christian individual and no Christian organization can be positive and constructive till *after* they have been negative and destructive. To deny or ignore this fact is to deny or ignore the fact of sin."[1] The negativism and pessimism of Ecclesiastes is directed at the humanistic assumption and total confidence that man has in his life and deeds. It indeed takes the fact of sin very seriously. The wisdom of God spoils the optimism of the would-be autonomous wisdom of sinful man. It demolishes the self-assurance with which secular man cherishes all his ideals. Ecclesiastes is a relentless discreditation of humanistic man, man in rebellion against God, and all that his life represents. It presents the clear assertion that God's law-word is the sum and substance of true wisdom. It's "gospel" proclaims that obedience to it "is the whole duty of man" (12:13). Anything less is "meaningless," for the end of man is death and judgment. All that he has done will be evaluated by his faithfulness to God's law-word. If he fails, he will have truly labored "in vain." Ecclesiastes contains a message that Christians as well need seriously to take into consideration. For Ecclesiastes also offers a solemn warning against the temptation to leave the paths of righteousness and to follow in the ways of worldly wisdom, which are the ways of vanity, meaninglessness, and death.

In Ecclesiastes the issue is joined between man's ways and God's way. The outcome of their confrontation is not in doubt. The pronouncement of "vanity of vanities" is not merely one of personal conviction on the part of the author; it is the verdict which he, under the guidance and inspiration of the Holy Spirit, renders on the would-be autonomous wisdom of fallen man. Ecclesiastes undermines every

1. Cornelius Van Til, *Essays On Christian Education*, (Phillipsburg: Presbyterian and Reformed Publishing Co., 1979), p.187.

prop on which we might count that does not take into consideration God and His sovereign Word. Its message is a vital one for our day.

Part I
The Context

I

Wisdom in Scripture

Nearly all modern scholars, liberal or conservative, readily classify Ecclesiastes as part of the "wisdom literature" of the religion of ancient Israel. To them this is the first and by far the most assured thing that one can say about it. Thus it is mainly viewed as the accomplishment of the religious genius of a onetime great and illustrious people. With Proverbs, Job and the Song of Solomon, Ecclesiastes is said to belong to a special cast of thinking and utterance that made up one tradition that, in combination with other traditions, contributed to the peculiar faith and values of the Hebrews. In other words, besides the Prophetic tradition with its prosecutory emphasis upon the law of Jehovah, and besides the Priestly tradition with its cult observances, we may speak of yet another tradition called "Wisdom" which early on (nobody can say for certain when) exercised an increasing influence upon the "scribes" and gradually, over the course of a few centuries, grew into a distinct and definable body of teaching having a major impact on the development of one of the great religions of ancient man. And, of course, by means of Judaism and Christianity that ancient wisdom has been passed on to us who have continued to reflect on its problems as well as its sententious prognoses for human experience in our own time. At least something along these lines is the way in which the wisdom heritage in the Scripture is seen by a Biblical scholarship too often controlled by the modern "enlightenment" spirit with its man-centered reconstruction of the Word of God.

In addition to being regarded as the product of the genius of a particular ancient people with its own unique blend of cultural and religious ideals, this peculiar Hebraic variety is thought to derive from shared values which sprang from some larger near-eastern and oriental world of religious and cultural wisdom. Dwelling as one nation in the midst of similar nations with similar traditions, Israel must surely have borrowed from that larger milieu as a source of inspiration, although the final product was tailored to her own circumstances and outlook. Not surprisingly, scholars have sought to explore the salient areas where they can compare wisdom in Israel to the more ancient ideals of the civilizations which surrounded her and which obviously went into the making of her own point of view. In this way the uniqueness of Biblical wisdom is regarded to be but a peculiar type of the general evolutionary development of ancient man and of his attempts to discover and define what is the distinctive quality of human life with its possibilities as well as limitations.

Now certainly, the great ancient civilizations, whether we think of Egypt or Mesopotamia—or even later of the Greek—possessed deeply held beliefs concerning wisdom as a useful guide to man for the achievement of the "good life," for that is what every wisdom tradition worthy of the name claims to provide. Of course, we cannot neglect to say something about those wisdom ideals which stood in contrast to the wisdom granted to Israel, but we shall reserve our comments for later, after we have clarified the nature and place of wisdom in Scripture. For the wisdom which was to have had exclusive claim on Israel could have no other source than almighty God, and it was deposited as Holy Writ.

This brings us to the heart of the matter. We do not for one moment regard the wisdom in Scripture to be a mere human contrivance that somehow consolidated progressively into a body of ideas which then acquired the authority of a venerated didactic custom—the accumulated wisdom of the ages, so to speak. Instead, Scriptural wisdom is a feature of God's redemptive revelation to His elect covenant people Israel. It was His gift, His special favor towards them to mark them off as peculiar and distinct from the nations around them. Israel was always to understand that her wisdom rested on her obedience to the righteous ordinances delivered to her through Moses, and on nothing else. She possessed what no nation had ever been privileged to possess: knowledge of the true and living God. In that knowledge she would grow into a wise people and become a beacon to the nations. Whatever wisdom existed in Israel was the fruit of God's calling of Israel to be His peculiar treasure and of having imparted to her an understanding of His Will. Unlike her neighbors who dwelt in darkness and ignorance, worshipping false gods and serving vain ideals—both the products of their sinful imagination—Israel was to live exclusively by a knowledge of a truth not of her own devising; one which was solely a gift of sovereign Divine grace.

The difference between the wisdom peculiar to Israel and the so-called wisdom of the great civilizations which surrounded, and sometimes attracted, her needs emphasis, especially as it relates to a study of Ecclesiastes. Because of its supposed negativism and pessimism, and its alleged stoical acquiescence in the face of a seemingly arbitrary fatalism, Ecclesiastes is routinely compared favorably to the wisdom models outside Israel. It is claimed that it adopts much of the same sentiment. How could it fail to be anything but a variety of ancient near-eastern wisdom in general? Even supposedly "conservative" scholars are reticent to admit that it contains, however vaguely, any "gospel" in its message. They, too, frequently interpret the book as pessimistic humanism. At the same time, they must admit, unlike their liberal preceptors, that Ecclesiastes does indeed belong in the canon of Scripture. But the hermeneutic they work with—man-centered for the most part—leaves them wondering just how it does fit there. Too often the writer of

Ecclesiastes is viewed as reflecting his own experience rather than speaking by inspiration of the Holy Spirit. In contrast, we maintain that a proper understanding of Ecclesiastes is connected to understanding the Biblical message as a whole. To recognize the Godly wisdom in Ecclesiastes will first require that we comprehend what wisdom means in Scripture generally.

It is a mistake to suppose that wisdom in Scripture resides exclusively in the so-called wisdom literature. Indeed, it is altogether wrong to think of wisdom as just a part of the Biblical message. Wisdom, rather, is the sum and substance of the Scriptural message in its entirety. Everything Scripture proclaims concerns wisdom. Every word is a word of wisdom, for Scripture "is able," says the apostle Paul, "to make you wise unto salvation through faith in Jesus Christ." (2 Tim. 3:15) Ecclesiastes is a book of wisdom only because it conveys, in its unique style and for its own distinct ends, the precise same wisdom message which issues from Scripture as a whole. It is "wisdom literature" because Scripture as such is "wisdom literature"; the part reflects the whole. Ecclesiastes is necessarily a part of the Scripture. If we desire to apprehend the wisdom content of Ecclesiastes, we shall need to know something of the nature, meaning and purpose of wisdom in Scripture more broadly. We will not succeed at getting at the heart of what Ecclesiastes teaches unless we are able to formulate a general doctrine of wisdom in Scripture. We begin where we are absolutely compelled to begin, with wisdom in relation to God Himself. Only by first considering what wisdom means in connection with God can we gain some appreciation of the rôle it is meant to play in the life and activity of man.

a. Wisdom and Creation

It is necessary to begin with God, for God is the Creator and man is His creature. Furthermore, God created man to be an exact replica of Himself, only on a finite scale.

Because man was fashioned after the image and likeness of God, to understand anything at all about man—the nature of his experience in the world, the purpose he was designed to fulfill—requires that we turn our thoughts in the first place towards God. If we begin by excluding God from our attempts to understand the life and being of man, as the modern world under the sway of Enlightenment ideals has undoubtedly done, then it is certain that we shall stray from the truth of Scripture. If man is but a finite analogy of the being and activity of God, then it is in the knowledge of God that the mystery of man will be revealed, including the place and practice of wisdom. Accordingly, whenever the Bible utters some truth about God and His deeds, it is a cue that we should pay attention, for it will have significance for our knowledge of man and his activity The Bible never merely provides information about God, however interesting in itself that may be. Rather, the knowledge and understanding it reveals about God is meant to teach an important truth about the life of man as well. Thus, by knowing God man can know himself.

In the matter of wisdom the Bible imparts crucial truth about God, hence about man. Let a few select passages exhibit what it teaches.

Proverbs declares, "By wisdom the Lord laid the earth's foundations, by understanding he set the heavens in place; by his knowledge the deeps were divided, and the clouds let drop the dew." (3:19f) Compare this with Jeremiah: "But God made the earth by his power; he founded the world by his wisdom and stretched out the heavens by his understanding." (10:12) Next to these two verses stands David's resonating tribute, "How many are your works, O Lord! In wisdom you made them all; the earth is full of your creatures." (Ps. 104:24) The stress in each of these verses lies on what God had done and how He had done it. In the first instance God created the heavens and the earth. This thought has become so ordinary in our minds that we fail to appreciate its significance. The work that is here attributed

to almighty God is not merely *a* work that He performed;
rather it is *the* work which God chose for Himself to accomplish. This task He appointed Himself to achieve, and He
completed it entirely on His own behalf and by His own
resources. It is His work. No other being could ever perform
this labor. He alone could do it; He alone willed to do it. He
was not compelled to do so, but He purposed to glorify
Himself by having done so. The chief thought is: God gave
Himself a job to do and He did it unto perfection. Notewor-
thy is the fact that God is a God who works; who consum-
mates purposes; who reaches goals; who realizes productive
accomplishments. Because God created man in His exact
image this thought will bear substantially upon the way that
we understand the nature and purpose of man's life in the
creation.

In the second place, it is equally necessary to apprehend
how God performed the work which He appointed for
Himself to achieve. In other words, what means did God
employ to complete the task? We learn that God worked
with the tools of wisdom, understanding, knowledge and
power. God was a careful builder; He acted from a well
thought-out plan of action. He perfectly calculated the
means that would realize the ends. His actions were not
guessed at nor did He hazard them to chance. Rather, He
thought profoundly about what He was doing and acted
from perfect wisdom and understanding.

In truth, the terms "wisdom," "understanding," and
"knowledge" are all interchangeable. This sheds light on
what is meant by wisdom. It is closely related to a capacity
of the mind: it possesses an intellectual component, not a
popular conception nowadays! Because of a mistaken pen-
chant for separating theory from practice we have come to
assume that they have no relationship to one another. But
intellectual insight can have profound repercussions for
practical experience. While wisdom is essentially practical
in nature, it is only so by the shaping and forming it has
received at the hands of sustained intellectual endeavor.

God is not an anti-intellect. He created the mind of man; He created the apparatus of logic as a tool for human thought—indeed, for the fulfillment of every human purpose. If the mind is not correctly nurtured and engaged, the practical side of life will suffer. Worse yet, under present sinful conditions man will find himself at the mercy of false conceptions of life and of the origin of truth; for the mind will involve itself in the world of man's experience whether we wish it or not. Even anti-intellectualism will be forced eventually to provide an "intellectual" justification.

So God worked His work with perfect wisdom. Understanding and knowledge are functional aspects of His wisdom. And the execution of His work—the power which He exercised—was in accordance with His wisdom, knowledge and understanding. It was not by mere power that God was able to accomplish His purpose, but by a power exercising a constructive insight into just how the job could be best performed and how the goals He had determined upon could be perfectly realized. The result was due to conception and plan.

From this thought we descend to man who was created to be like God. The person and activity of God are man's exemplars. Therefore, since God works, man too was created to work and achieve productive ends or goals. Moreover, man was meant to realize his labor in the same manner as God Himself had done, by means of wisdom, knowledge and understanding. God's work is self-determined but man's work is determined by God. Only He Whose work is self-determined could be the original Creator of the world; yet, as the determiner of man's work, God has given to man the responsibility to "re-create" that which God had originally created. The idea here is one of analogy. Man cannot create as God did. However, on a finite scale, he too was meant to be a builder of his world and in this sense would model his behavior after God's. This thought emerges in Gen. 1:26,28 where God commands man to have dominion over the earth. It expresses the requirement that he should build God's kingdom on earth. To complete the task God endowed man with the same tools that He Himself possessed, only once again in accordance with the created nature of man. Wisdom, knowledge and understanding were original characteristics of man, not something to which he would attain. These were the spiritual and intellectual equipment that would be needed by him in order to do what God required of him. If man expected to be successful in the performance of his calling, if he was to be "empowered" in reaching his goal, then he could not dispense with precisely the instruments that God Himself employed to succeed in His work.

From the Biblical viewpoint, then, wisdom was an original feature of the life and nature of man in the work he was created to perform and gets its meaning solely from that goal. Apart from that endeavor it possesses no significance. Wisdom (knowledge and understanding) was not merely for the sake of having but for the sake of doing. Man should have been as successful in his enterprise as God was in His. The tragedy of his failure stems from his willful rebellion against God and from his refusal to have anything to do with God's purpose for his life.

The Fall into sin has had a devastating impact upon man's wisdom. In Scripture there are two essential lines of thought that clarify the problem of wisdom in man as a result of sin. First, Scripture wishes to make undeniably clear that man's wisdom has become thoroughly corrupted and perverted in consequence of man's disobedience. So much so that it does not go too far to say that man has virtually ceased to possess even a shred of sound wisdom. It does not deny that a capacity for wisdom (and knowledge and understanding) continues to reside in man, for if man were to lose even the potential for wisdom he would cease to be man in any sense. Recall that man was made in God's image, and that wisdom, knowledge and understanding were indispensable aspects of image-of-God. What Scripture does affirm is the utter perversity of wisdom now in man. The need to live life "wisely," as it were, does not cease to impress its demand upon the consciousness of sinful man; only now because the heart has undergone a profound moral and religious change the wisdom which guides him is radically misdirected.

In the Garden man chose a wisdom other than God's and he must now live with the consequences of a false wisdom. His whole conception of life and purpose will be rooted in and will issue from this false wisdom. He will seek to realize his ideal of the kingdom of man in terms of it, but he will find that because of the curse God has laid on him he will constantly experience frustration in his desire. It is this inescapable truth that adds poignancy to the Preacher's lamentation at the very outset of his work, when he asks, "What does man gain from all his labor at which he toils under the sun?" (Eccles. 1:3) He knows what the answer is, as well as why. He gains nothing! Man has turned aside from God, the only true source of sound wisdom and has sought after a wisdom thought to be self-generated from the consciousness of man alone. The correlation of wisdom, knowledge and understanding to power is greatly attenuated and vastly askew because of man's sin. Yet man continues to believe that he is in possession of a wisdom that will enable him to overcome this fundamental discrepancy. It is part and parcel to the wisdom message of Scripture to make us face up to this delusion.

Second, if sound wisdom is to be recovered in man so that man might once again know what is truly good for himself and acquire the needed capability to implement that good in his life and culture, man must be redeemed from his false ideal of wisdom. God must restore in man true wisdom, knowledge and understanding. Man must come to recognize his need for this restoration. This is the greatest concern of the wisdom message in Scripture, that basic to God's work is His program of reclamation of the true image of Himself in man. The work of God in redemption can never be disconnected from the work of God in creation.

God wishes man again to work the work which God gave
him to do. To impress this on man's consciousness he must
be made to see that the false wisdom by which he now lives
is entirely futile. That is why Ecclesiastes repeatedly drives
home the point of the meaninglessness and vanity of everything that man does under the sun.

b. Wisdom and Redemption

Scripture teaches plainly that, besides fashioning man in
His own image in order for man to work and to build His
kingdom on earth, God intended that man should be His
companion and enjoy fellowship with Himself. A personal
communion between God and man rested at the heart of
God's creation program. The whole of man's life was cen-
tered on this "covenant" relationship. The original
attributes of wisdom, knowledge and understanding could
mean nothing for man if they did not include the wisdom,
knowledge and understanding of God Himself. Fundamental to the Scriptural doctrine of wisdom is the notion of asso-
ciation with God in His holiness, righteousness and truth.
Man could not expect to fulfill his calling to have dominion
if he sought it in separation from partnership with God. No
wisdom remained possible for man apart from a wisdom in
the ways of God first and foremost. It is impossible rightly to
understand the bearing which redemption has on wisdom,
as Scripture conceives it, without apprehending the original
situation of man as God intended it, for the restoration of
true wisdom, knowledge and understanding in man is con-
tingent upon a recovery of the lost communion with God.

The wisdom (knowledge and understanding) concerning
God which man possessed at creation could not have been
attained by man on his own; it was implanted in his soul by
God. Man came into the world endowed with a true knowledge of God; however, it was not a developed and mature
knowledge, but needed to be brought to fruition. To achieve
that goal God spoke to man and told him what He would

demand of him. In other words, God addressed him with a law-word as the stipulation for all his activity. It was made plain to him that his wisdom, in every respect, would depend upon a faithful adherence to God's word. If he obeyed he would merit eternal life; if he refused to obey, if he transgressed God's command, he would merit eternal punishment. Man opted for disobedience and as a result has reaped the consequences of the loss of true wisdom, knowledge and understanding.

Yet Scripture is clear when it claims that God determined, from before the foundations of the earth, to deliver and redeem man from the death he has so justly deserved as a result of his rebellion against God's will. This program of redemption was announced at the beginning and unfolded gradually in the course of man's history. At its core stands the calling and formation of a people who will learn to call on God's name and once again proceed to base all of life on the solid foundation of His word. Scripture claims to be that word. The recovery of sound wisdom, knowledge and understanding is conditioned upon the faithful response to its message and obedience to its truth alone. Without the light of Scripture man walks in darkness and perverts the truth. We are unavoidably compelled to submit to its authority and to heed its admonition.

In the first place, Scripture teaches that wisdom is a function of righteousness, and righteousness a function of God's law. No other possible basis for wisdom exists. Scripture is adamant on this point. The acquisition of wisdom cannot be seen as the result of a vague adherence to some supposed good "as such" as, for example, Plato envisioned it. Man is altogether without any idea of what is truly good. He must be told by God what is good, and God's word says plainly that he is a wise man who lives in accordance with His statutes and precepts: "The law of the Lord is perfect, reviving the soul. The statutes of the Lord are trustworthy, making wise the simple." (Ps. 19:7)

Law observance should not be viewed, however, as the

mere mechanical application of duty to an external command. On the contrary, unless it takes root in the heart and
springs from genuine fidelity to God it is not a Biblical righteousness. At the core of law-obedience throbs a pulsating
"fear of the Lord"—a sense that God has the right to define
the ethical parameters of one's life, to dictate the terms that
shape one's entire philosophy of life. "The fear of the Lord
is the beginning [i.e., fountain or wellspring] of wisdom; all
who follow his precepts have good understanding." (Ps.
111:10) "The fear of the Lord is the beginning [i.e., heart's
motive] of wisdom, and knowledge of the Holy One is
understanding." (Prov. 9:10) God's people were told that
they must not fail to understand that it was God's law in
their lives that would mark them off from the nations as a
wise people (Deut. 4:5-8). Their "greatness" would be the
reward of their wisdom. The exaltation of their reputation
and the dominance of their power would follow as a result
of their faithful submission to God's law-order. Wisdom in
Scripture is inescapably a property of righteousness. If the
mouth of the righteous man utters wisdom, and if his
tongue speaks what is just, it is only because God's law has
taken hold in his heart (Ps. 37:30f). To seek a wisdom apart
from God's law is a vain enterprise. It is the burden of
Ecclesiastes to convey precisely this thought. Its outcry of
"vanity, vanity, all is vanity!" means nothing less.

But, in the second place it is important to note that this
truth does not imply that wisdom is not a gift of God's
grace. Adherence to God's law as the directive of one's
entire life does not earn wisdom for oneself; rather, law
observance is the fruit of a wisdom that God grants to man
in grace and redemption. Scripture clearly teaches that
whatever wisdom man possesses comes to him from God.
"For the Lord gives wisdom, and from his mouth come
knowledge and understanding." (Prov. 2:6) "I will guide you
in the way of wisdom and lead you in straight paths." (Prov.
4:11) Wisdom is plainly a benefit of Divine benevolence and
counsel. No wisdom exists for man other than that incul-

cated by God Himself (Ps. 51:6). More than this, Scripture claims that the presence of wisdom in man derives from the presence in him of God's Spirit. Deuteronomy 34:9 declares that Joshua was fitted for the task of kingdom leadership and conquest because he had been filled with the Spirit of Wisdom. The reference here is undoubtedly to the Holy Spirit and distinguishes the manner in which eventually all God's people can expect to prosper in the pathway of wisdom and understanding, and so too in accomplishment. To the extent that God's Spirit dwells in his people they can walk in wisdom. This thought, too, is not missing from Ecclesiastes, though its appearance there is less overt, more implied.

A third feature of the Scriptural doctrine of wisdom is the distinction which it asserts between the wise man and the fool. These categories correspond to the difference between the man who walks in the fear of the Lord—according to His law-word—and the man who does not. In other words, it elucidates what separates the way of the righteous from that of the sinner. It is the only distinction between men that Scripture recognizes. All other differences (e.g., race, nationality, sex, etc.) are, in the matter of wisdom, irrelevant. Time and again one encounters words like these: "The fear of the Lord is the beginning of knowledge, but fools despise wisdom and discipline." (Prov. 1:7) "The lips of the righteous nourish many, but fools die for lack of judgment. A fool finds pleasure in evil conduct, but a man of understanding delights in wisdom." (Prov. 10:21, 23) "A wise man fears the Lord and shuns evil, but a fool is hotheaded and reckless. The simple inherit folly, but the prudent are crowned with knowledge." (Prov. 14:16, 18) "Folly delights a man who lacks judgment, but a man of understanding keeps a straight course." (Prov. 15:21) "Understanding is a fountain of life to those who have it, but folly brings punishment to fools." (Prov. 16:22)

In the view of Scripture all of life resolves itself into one or the other, with no third type of man, for every man is either a covenant keeper or a covenant breaker. What he is will determine whether he is wise or foolish.

The fool is everything that the wise man is not. "Fool" is a general term to describe one or all of the subsequent designations: wicked, evil speaker, deceiver, liar, slanderer, cheat, greedy, lazy, haughty, arrogant, boastful, unstable, untrustworthy, simple-minded (i.e., incapable of true discernment), to mention but a few. He is some of these things or all of them because he refuses to submit to God and His law-word. It is advisable to take careful note of the fool, for the actions of the fool have deleterious consequences. The fool destroys life; he does not build it up. The harm he does affects not only himself but society as well. His behavior is the cause of everyone's ruin and loss. When fools triumph, life becomes short, mean, nasty, and brutish. Not surprisingly, Scripture is urgent in its warning against the dangers of folly. The fool's life is, and always has been, the single greatest hindrance to the achievement of dominion and the realization of God's kingdom purpose for man. He stands as the enemy of the wise. Jesus will have something important to say concerning the wise man and the fool (Matt. 7:24-27). He will make the doing of His word to be the sole criterion by which to distinguish between the fool and the wise man. Of this, more in a later chapter.

Every doctrine of wisdom immediately involves a notion of its opposite. Since covenant-breaking man claims to possess an ideal of wisdom, he, too, necessarily distinguishes between the wise man and the fool. Each of the major civilizations which flourished in proximity to Israel presumed to offer a wisdom message. Each of these included ideas of what would not be in conformity to the wisdom ideal it presented, and so what would be bad for man. Non-christian man at the present time continues to hold to an ideal of wisdom that, in his estimation, stands preeminent over anything that does not conform to his promise of the good life. But, we should understand clearly that, whatever division separates the wise man from the fool in the pagan consciousness, it has nothing to do with whether or not a man is righteous in accordance with God's law-word. It is altogether a man-centered conception.

In the West, we have had to live to a great extent with a humanistic (i.e., God-opposed) notion of "the good" that took its origins from the Greeks and which has sought increasingly to control the direction of cultural formation throughout our history. One of the most influential founders of this humanistic tradition was the philosopher Plato whose thought contains a self-consciously developed concept of wisdom for man. Plato's, and persistently western humanistic man's, view has been an exclusively intellectualist and elitist conception of wisdom. Wisdom for him is identical with an autonomous *scientia*, or what he termed *theoria*. Wisdom is strictly a matter of following the dictates of a divine reason!—a reason not in the least contaminated by man's fall into sin, not having need then to submit to any ethical authority other than itself.

Not every person, however, can be in possession of "science", only those especially endowed by nature and training. Since without it man does not have wisdom, the presumption arises that where wisdom (science) is absent, there foolishness must automatically fill the void. Nature distributes this her greatest gift only to a select few. Ultimately, Plato's distinction between the wise man and the fool was metaphysical, not ethical. Fools could never themselves expect to be wise. And since the man of wisdom alone could provide an insight into the good life, the fool must be made (by political power) to submit to the guidance of the expert wise. The latter's superior knowledge must give him the right to be in charge of ordering all society to follow his blueprint. Such an elitist idea of wisdom has led all humanists after Plato to treat with contempt anyone not thought to be in possession of its attributes, i.e., not holding membership in the priviledged circle of the initiates. Plato held the non-philosopher in low esteem because not having access to "holy philosophy" such a one was less than true man.

In contrast to this pagan conception Scripture never
speaks superciliously or disparagingly of the fool. God does
not regard the fool as beneath His contempt. The problem
of the fool is religious and ethical, not metaphysical. Men do
not cease to be image-of-God just because foolishness has
implanted itself in their consciousness and behavior. It is not
because a man is a non-philosopher that he is a fool.
Besides, a wise man has nothing in and of himself that
would, before God, give him a just claim to boast. All men,
after Adam made his foolish choice, are born with the
nature of a fool indelibly printed on their souls. If we are
wise, it is only by the grace of God and by the faithful submission to His sovereign word. Foolishness and wisdom are
like poverty and wealth: the former is what every man is
born into, it is the normal state of affairs for anyone who has
since the Fall ever lived; on the other hand, wisdom like
wealth must be produced and achieved by great exertion
and in the face of the constant threat of poverty and foolishness.

Unless God had condescended to act on our behalf in
mercy and redemption we would have had to suffer forever
the consequences of our foolishness. But by His grace and
compassion we are enabled once again to find true wisdom.
Thus, if God contemns anything it is the attitude which pre-
tends to wisdom and superiority over others when in fact
such boastfulness is itself the highest form of vainglorious
foolishness. Accordingly, with scarcely concealed anger
Proverbs exclaims, "Do you see a man wise in his own eyes?
There is more help for a fool than for him." (26:12) The
Lord can abide a fool, for it is possible that an ordinary fool
will recognize himself for what he is and will turn in repentance and trust toward God; but, when the heart becomes
calloused and utterly blind to its true condition, when it
actually believes itself in possession of a wisdom it does not
have, then, as Scripture indicates, that man has passed
beyond any help and is deserving only of God's wrath. It is
an indication of this that a man trusts in his own righteous-

ness and feels himself justified in his own sight. Consequently, Scripture issues an urgent warning, "Woe to those who are wise in their own eyes and clever in their own sight." (Isa. 5:21) The great problem for God's people has persistently been that they have shown a willingness to adopt the pagan conception and to deny that it is God's law alone that must act as the standard of wise thought and conduct. "These people come near me with their mouth and honor me with their lips, but their hearts are far from me. Their worship of me is made up only of rules taught by men." (Isa. 29:13) Men's rules can never substitute for God's law as a legitimate ideal of wisdom. If our worship is perverted our lives and service will be perverted as well. Clearly, wisdom lies in the way of doing God's will and not in the confidence that man has in himself. It will be the purpose of Ecclesiastes to drive this thought home with inescapable clarity.

II

The Wisdom of Solomon

Unquestionably central to the Biblical doctrine of wisdom is the wisdom of Solomon. All that has significance for the former comes to its glorious realization and confirmation in the latter. Scripture furnishes no wisdom message that does not at the same time offer a living example in the Man of Wisdom himself. Solomonic wisdom displays the living presence of the whole Scriptural ideal and points to its foremost representative both in creation and in redemption. In this respect, Solomon cannot be viewed as a man who merely happened to be wise; rather the wisdom he possessed and exercised had as its purpose to promote the covenant headship principle in Scripture. In connection with *creation* Solomon refers back to Adam and to the situation that God had originally purposed for man. In connection with *redemption* Solomon looks ahead to and anticipates, in his person and accomplishments, the advent of Christ in whom shall ultimately be found hidden all the treasures of wisdom and knowledge (Col. 2:3). Solomon's wisdom and rôle must be viewed, then, in their redemptive-historical context. It is this thought, too, which must govern our understanding of the book of Ecclesiastes, for it claims unequivocally to speak from the standpoint of the Solomonic wisdom.

The passage in Scripture that is key to grasping the extraordinary dimensions of the wisdom associated with the historical Solomon is I Kgs. 3:12, "I will give you a wise and discerning heart, so that there will never have been anyone like you, nor will there ever be." Plainly, Solomon's wisdom belongs in a special category. It is not a wisdom that just anyone could hope to acquire for himself. Neither before nor after Solomon does any *mere* man compare in the matter of wisdom. Solomon's wisdom is therefore unique. His wisdom exemplifies that of the covenant head: it is the wisdom of Adam that was lost; it is the wisdom of Christ that God has been historically in the process of bringing to its realization. By exalting Solomon in the matter of wisdom God was making it evident that true wisdom (knowledge and understanding) would be grounded and brought to fruition in the Man that He would choose to set over His people Israel— indeed, over the nations. In Solomon would become spectacularly apparent all the wisdom of God Himself. All would come to see that Solomon's kingly dominion and achievement was the consequence and outgrowth of a wisdom that was not like anything man had ever seen or heard, nor could possibly hope to attain to by the ordinary application of learning. It was simply not to be found in man in any sense.

It must be stressed that Solomon's gift of wisdom—for a gift it most certainly was and not something of which even Solomon could boast was a facet of "natural" genius — stood on the foundation of faithful covenant obedience to God and His righteousness. For, in I Kings it is made clear to Solomon that the favor he enjoyed in the matter of wisdom rested on the responsibility he was given of living in accordance with the righteous ordinances handed down to him from his father David—"if you walk in *my ways* and obey my statues and commands as David your father did." (I Kgs. 3:14) Earlier David himself had solemnly entreated Solomon to continue steadfast in what the Lord God requires: "Walk in his ways, and keep his decrees and commands, his laws and requirements, as written in the Law of Moses, so that you may prosper in all you do and wherever you go...." (I Kgs. 2:3) Solomon's wisdom, and the stupendous benefits that would accrue to him by it, were conditional upon a careful observance to obey every word which proceeds from the mouth of God. This was how Adam was to have lived in God's world; it is how Christ alone succeeded in living *in* the world. Solomon's wisdom and the place it occupies in Scripture was meant to reflect the full implications of the total doctrine of wisdom that we sketched in the last chapter. In his wisdom is summed up all the wisdom of Scripture as it comes to full fruition in kingdom service.

I Kgs. 4:33f summarily exhibits both the Adamic and Christological characteristics of Solomon's peculiar wisdom. The first comes necessarily to the forefront in verse 33: "He described plant life, from the cedar of Lebanon to the hyssop that grows out of walls. He taught about animals and birds, and reptiles and fish." One is reminded of the work of naming the animals which Adam performed in Gen. 2:19f. That labor was to be the prelude to Adam's subsequent task of exercising dominion over all the earth. By having first acquired knowledge of the realm of nature Adam would then be properly and adequately fitted for his exalted responsibility. In like manner, Solomon demonstrates that his practice of kingship was rooted in a systematic knowledge of the total realm of nature. In the second place, his rule extended to the world of man and his concerns. Here his wisdom displayed a ready insight into all things human. "Men of all nations came to listen to Solomon's wisdom, sent by all the kings of the world, who had heard of his wisdom." (v.34) With this thought, Scripture conveys more distinctly the Christological features of Solomon's wisdom and reign. For in a fallen world the wretched disturbances in the life of man and society have assumed the gravest proportions. Solomon's wisdom necessarily takes on the features of a redemptive and restorative proclamation. It sets forth the law of God as the only possible solution to the inevitable degeneracy of the communities of men. By coming to hear the wisdom of Solomon, the nations give testimony to the bankruptcy of the kingdom of man as well as recognition of the incomparable superiority of the Biblical wisdom as the correct pathway of justice, peace, and prosperity. Solomon's wisdom was salve and balm for countless difficulties that attend the circumstances of fallen human existence.

No greater vindication of this Solomonic truth can be discovered in the writings of Solomon himself than in the expansive petition which we read in Psalm 72. From the very first moment Solomon recognized that his possession of wisdom was not for his personal benefit alone, but was meant to serve the greater purposes of God and His kingdom. His wisdom is the product of being endowed exclusively with God's justice (v.1). Its true nature therefore is to implement God's will according to His law with no other idea of justice than that which God commands in His Word. By no other possible means could Solomon judge the people in righteousness (v.2)—a people who did not belong to Solomon but rather to God. Nor could he properly defend the afflicted, nor save the children of the needy, nor crush the oppressor (v.4) if he had any notion of doing so other than by what God's word requires. It was this success of God's law-word in the reign of the Man of Wisdom that would bring with it the abundant outpouring of God's blessing upon the people as a whole. "In his days the righteous will flourish; prosperity will abound till the moon is no more." (v.7) The exaltation of Solomonic wisdom redounded to the astonishing well-being of Israel, and it is this triumphant fact which brings the nations to bow down and serve Solomon (v.11). They cannot help but recognize that the way of the Lord is good for all men everywhere and naturally desire to get in on this good thing. All these things had their preliminary realization in the period of the historic Solomon. Yet their ultimate manifestation awaited the arrival of that Greater Solomon—Jesus Christ—of whom the historic Solomon was but a type and precursor. The glory of Solomon's limited days must give way to the greater glory of the endless days of the Son of Man.

The wisdom of Solomon stands for a complete civiliza-

tional program. It represents the way of life of a total culture
and is not merely of personal significance. Because
Solomon's wisdom is not of his own invention, but is a
divine endowment, it cannot apply to him alone. It is a wisdom that was meant to enhance the greater goals of the
Kingdom of God. It reflects the elevation of that Kingdom
in the world, and its entire purpose is to augment that Kingdom and to work for its conquest over every aspect of man's
life and society. But sinful man desires an alternative kingdom—the kingdom of man. He necessarily proffers an altogether different wisdom program than that found in God's
law-word, claiming that his, not God's, will redound to the
greater happiness of mankind. The wisdom ideal he
embraces is the intellectual and moral means by which he
seeks to make legitimate and to promote the cultural and
civilizational principles of the kingdom for which he longs
and in which he most sincerely believes. Since these two
kingdoms are antithetical and therefore involve an unavoidable clash of interests, the wisdom ideals for which each
stands are equally opposed. One or the other must achieve
the victory. In I Kgs. 4:30 we read: "Solomon's wisdom was
greater than the wisdom of all the men of the East, and
greater than all the wisdom of Egypt." The reference is not
merely to Solomon personally, but includes the civilizational
goals which his wisdom advocates. It is not just a personal
triumph for Solomon; more than this, it refers to the triumph of the Kingdom of God over the kingdom of man.
The victory of the Solomonic wisdom and the conquest of
the Kingdom of God are inescapably involved in one
another.

At this point we must understand the cultural and civilizational ideals that stood in opposition to Israel throughout
her history and which in the end entirely absorbed her in
their pagan outlook. After all, Israel departed from her
Solomonic (i.e., Biblical) wisdom heritage and followed false
gods with the false cultural principles that they represented.
If we fail to understand this clash of civilizational values

then the message of Ecclesiastes is bound to seem an enigma.

The two major civilizations which represented the kingdom of man in the history of the Old Testament were those of the East, or Mesopotamia (Assyria or Babylonia), and of Egypt. Each civilization presented itself as a rival to Israel, and each had a vision of absolute world domination. No doubt Mesopotamia and Egypt differed from one another, and no doubt each fought with the other to claim the crown rights of the kingdom of man. But the difference between the two is insignificant when both are compared with the principles and ideals which were to govern the society and life of God's people. Humanistic men may not always agree with one another, but all remain united against God and His Kingdom. Aristotle and Plato may appear to stand for different ideas and explanations of things, but both are in agreement that what God says is fundamentally false. These two civilizations, then, offered a serious challenge to the covenant people of God. They were a threat not solely by reason of the military might by which they physically subdued nations and peoples, but more especially because they offered an attractive alternate righteousness, and hence "good," to Israel than that which was expressed by the law of God.[1] It is essential to examine the central features of their respective cultural and civilizational ideals.

a. Egypt

Secular scholars have debated the question of which civilization is the older—the civilization of the Nile valley, or that of the Tigris-Euphrates valley—but for our purpose it is not important except to say that, as far as Scripture is concerned, both began at roughly the same time, i.e., shortly after the Great Flood, when mankind was dispersed over the face of the earth. Still, it is true that at a much earlier

---

1. See, Rousas John Rushdoony, *Thy Kingdom Come: Studies in Daniel and Revelation*, (Fairfax, Thoburn Press, 1978), p.27.

time in the history of Israel Egypt was the nation with which
she first came into contact and conflict; for this reason, we
begin with Egypt.

In the ancient world—and in the ancient existence of
God's people—the great clash of interests which emerged
between the Kingdom of God and the kingdom of man took
place at the highest level in man's thinking. It was nothing
less than a conflict between *God* and *the gods*: the worship of
false gods versus the worship of the true and living God.
When Israel was rescued out of Egyptian bondage, at the
core of the revelation that God had entrusted to her
appeared the warning about false gods. Ex. 20:22 states,
"Tell the Israelites this: 'You have seen for yourselves that I
have spoken to you from heaven: Do not make any gods to
be alongside me; do not make for yourselves gods of silver or
gods of gold'." Every issue, every difference between the civilizations in contention originates from and turns upon this
central religious confrontation. So, too, when it comes to
wisdom, understanding and knowledge, an inescapable connection exists between them and the religious perspective at
the center of the civilization which they represent and seek
to promote.

To put the problem this way, however, can give rise to a
misconception. For although the primary issue at stake at
the highest level in the ancient world was a confrontation
between the *One* True God and the *many* false gods of the
pagan world of thought, it would be a mistake to assume
that the matter resolved itself into a dispute between theological monotheism and theological polytheism pure and
simple. The true nature of the affair goes much deeper than
this. As touching the matter of wisdom in particular Jeremiah has put his finger squarely on the problem: "Among all
the wise men of the nations and in all their kingdoms, there
is no one like you. They are all senseless and foolish; they
are taught by worthless wooden idols." (10:7, 8) To Jeremiah
it is not so much a matter of monotheism versus polytheism
as it is the consequences for man when he so stubbornly and

foolishly persists in his bold attempt to erase the *Creator-creature* distinction. This is what truly stands at the heart of all the false religions of man; polytheism is merely the form that religion takes when man endeavors to wipe out the difference between God the Creator and himself as the creature. It also indicates the vast gulf which lies between the Solomonic wisdom and the wisdom of the two opposing cultures of Egypt and Babylon. Both alike stand for the utter destruction of the distinction between the Creator and creature, for by this they both hope to make succeed the Satanic asseveration—"you shall be as God knowing good and evil." (Gen. 3:5) By demolishing the difference between God and man humanistic man thinks that it is possible to discover a way by which man can come to participate in the nature of divinity itself. By bringing God within the same cosmos of experience as man, man imagines that he can be raised to the same level with God and so proclaim both himself and his endeavors to be divine and everlasting.

This view of things is the pivotal conception in the culture and civilization of ancient Egypt. To an Egyptian "between god and man there was no point at which one could erect a boundary line and state that here substance changed from divine, superhuman, immortal, to mundane, human, mortal."[2] There simply was "no firm and final dividing-line between gods and men."[3] Consequently, no firm difference in nature obtained between gods and men. Both alike participated in the same cosmos of existence, binding men and gods in the same continuity of experience. At most, the rôle of divinity was meant to provide man with a paradigm, an archetype[4], for every human activity within the boundaries of a common law of nature. The sacred and

2. John A. Wilson in H. and H.A. Frankfort, John A. Wilson, Thorkild Jacobsen, *Before Philosophy: The Intellectual Adventure of Ancient Man*, (Baltimore: Penguin Books, 1964), p.75.
3. *Before Philosophy*, p.64.
4. See, for example, Mircea Eliade, *The Myth of the Eternal Return*, trans. by Willard R. Trask, (New York: Princeton University Press/Bollingen Foundation Incorporated, 1974).

the eternal provided a model to be actualized in the realm
of the profane and the temporal. There is no concept of creation "ex nihilo" in Egyptian thinking, for that would imply
that divinity transcends the cosmos of experience which
delimits the life of man—and not only transcends the universe but ultimately stands responsible for its very existence.
Any idea of creation in Egyptian thought refers to nothing
more than the arrangement of the stuff of experience for
both gods and men. At best the gods might bring order out
of a pre-existing chaos. Even so, order does not imply permanence or perfection. For the possibility always looms that
the primordial chaos might reverse the work of the gods and
once again defeat order and harmony.

The anxiety which this threat produced in the mind of
the ancient Egyptian was palpable and constant. In general,
he could never be certain that the providence of his gods
was a security against the total ruination which would be his
in such a catastrophe. He was encouraged to believe that
the only guarantee of the order and regularity of his experience depended upon the formation of an inclusive cosmic
society of gods and men, of heaven and earth. In his system
of beliefs the most important concern was to be fully integrated into the life of nature and "the experience of that
harmony was thought to be the greatest good to which man
could aspire."[5] The achievement of this goal was imagined
to lie in the Egyptian idea of the state with its god-man king
at the center as the mediator between heaven and earth. A
state-dominated society with an infallible monarch lay at
the heart of the civilizational program of ancient Egypt.

The concept of the state was a necessary corollary in the
total cosmic ideal of ancient Egyptian culture and religion.
And central to the idea of the state was the divinity of the
King. "The state was not a man-made alternative to other
forms of political organization. It was god-given...it continued to form part of the universal order. In the person of the

5. Henri Frankfort, *Ancient Egyptian Religion*, (New York: Harper & Brothers,
   1961), p.29.

Pharaoh a super-human being had taken charge of the affairs of man."[6] The king did not merely exercise rule; he was responsible for maintaining the harmony of the cosmos. The onslaught of the powers of chaos were an ever recurring threat. The king embodied in his person the equilibrium between Seth and Horus, Strife and Order. This antagonism was permanent and without resolution. Yet, because the king was both at once, he somehow maintained peace between them.[7] In consequence, "the service of Pharaoh was a religious, not a purely secular, function, and sense of duty was strengthened by faith."[8] The ancient Egyptian's culture was a slave culture, one of absolute servitude to the power and authority of the king. In his scheme of things it represented his hope of redemption. The fiat word of the Pharaoh could brook no opposition. The life of the Egyptian was in the hand of his king as in the hand of his god.

The Egyptians had a word to describe the cosmic concept of order which they imagined to exist and which they supposed their king was ordained to uphold. They called it Ma'at. Often the word has been translated as "truth," or "justice," but its correct meaning is more that of "right order."[9] To live in accordance with Ma'at—right order—meant, for every Egyptian, to live the best life possible. That man who lives in tune with Ma'at is therefore a *wise* man.

The Egyptian deeply feared the possible return of chaos and disorder, the complete overthrow of all normality and regularity. The establishment of order, he hoped, would be a permanent bulwark against such a recurrence. If change anywhere in nature should occur he could be certain that chaos was responsible and was determined to regain its previous domination. True order must not only be permanent but static and changeless. The notion of history or progress

6. Frankfort, *Ancient Egyptian Religion*, p. 30.
7. Henri Frankfort, *Kingship and the Gods*, (Chicago: The University of Chicago Press, 1984), p. 22.
8. Frankfort, *Ancient Egyptian Religion*, p. 45.
9. Frankfort, *Kingship and the Gods*, p. 51.

was foreign to his thinking. Indeed, to believe that man and society should undergo development and growth was the most profound heresy. It is not strange, then, that his conception of Ma'at (right order) should be viewed more in terms of what it is *not*, than of what it is; that he should be more concerned with what threatened to destroy it than with what justifies its nature and existence. Ma'at has been established. That is axiomatic. The wise man will live so as not to upset the rule of right order. He will bow in humble submission to Ma'at. He will submit unreservedly to his god-king.

Whoever lives in accordance with Ma'at will flourish and prosper, but "whoever acts against Ma'at comes ultimately to grief."[10] To the Egyptian this was an article of faith. A ready formula was provided for every manifestation of good or evil in a man's life. Every eventuality had a predictable explanation by reason of this moral prescription. Actions which necessarily disturbed the right order of the cosmos must inevitably prove harmful and cause grievous injury to man. What possible factor could inspire man to act so contrary to his own best interests? It was a lack of correct insight or proper self-restraint, and not some basic corruption within man, that accounted for man's misfortunes.[11] "The Egyptian viewed his misdeeds not as sins, but as aberrations."[12] He was not concerned so much that his behavior was morally wrong as that it brought him unhappiness. In particular the fault belonged to his "passions" or "emotions" which were a residue of chaos in his nature, something for which he was not to be blamed. Still it was within his power to prevent. If a man chose to live by his irrational impulses and desires, then his willful lack of self-control was certain to bring him misery. However, "he who errs was not a sinner but a fool, and his conversion to a better way of life does not require repentance but a better understanding."[13]

10. Frankfort, *Ancient Egyptian Religion*, p.62.
11. Frankfort, *Ancient Egyptian Religion*, p.74.
12. Frankfort, *Ancient Egyptian Religion*, p. 73.

Here we encounter his doctrine of wisdom. "True wisdom...means mastery over one's impulses.... One must be
able to avoid getting involved in situations in which one is
likely to be carried away by one's feelings." "Restraint of
passions and an avoidance of extremes in general, characterize the wise man."[14] Hubris, or pride, was another agent
working against the good life. It meant the "loss of the sense
of proportion, a self-reliance, a self-assertion which passed
the bounds of man and hence led to disaster."[15] Simply put,
Ma'at was an order that could not be violated with impu-
nity. The Egyptian felt the heavy daily burden of organizing
every activity in accordance with its inviolable command.
He could not be certain moment by moment which act
would transgress its rule and so bring violent retribution
upon him.

Nevertheless, Ma'at expresses no specific ethical com-
mandment. The opposite of Ma'at is not injustice or
unrighteousness, but chaos. Ma'at even determines the
order of the gods. They, too, are bound by Ma'at, and are
liable to its revenge if they should overstep its borders. Quite
simply, it was a cosmic force of the first order, nothing stood
higher. Naturally, when men erred they were not commit-
ting sins against the gods but they moved against the established order of things. Men are not viewed in rebellion
against God, nor, in the final analysis, does wisdom come
from God or reflect the will of God, but it is strictly human
in nature.[16]

The comparison of the Egyptian view of things—its civilizational outlook—with that of Solomon and the Biblical
view is obvious. In like manner, the Solomonic world-view
contrasts with that of ancient Mesopotamia.

13. Frankfort, *Ancient Egyptian Religion*, p 73.
14. Frankfort, *Ancient Egyptian Religion*, p. 66, 68.
15. Frankfort, *Ancient Egyptian Religion*, p. 69.
16. Frankfort, *Ancient Egyptian Religion*, pp. 76, 77, 81.

b. Mesopotamia

As did Egypt, Mesopotamia stood for an integrated and self-contained civilizational ideal.[17] Mesopotamian man, like his opposite number in Egypt, was deeply possessed of a total cosmic outlook on life, encompassing at once the lowest peasant and the highest gods. And once again, in the middle stood the office of the king which represented the bond between heaven and earth.[18] Not surprisingly, we also observe that a state-dominated, totalitarian society presented the appearance of the greatest good for all forms of life within the same cosmos of experience. The reason, one discovers, as it was with the Egyptian, is that the Mesopotamian desperately desired and believed in the reign of order over the tyranny of chaos. The trouble is, his entire conception of order was itself nothing less than despotic and as a result filled him, at best, with a dreaded sense of a dismal fate. In this respect, he was much less sanguine than his Egyptian counterpart; yet, no less willing to accede to the ideals and beliefs which his civilization represented.

The ancient Mesopotamian looked at life as essentially an ineradicable conflict. The world order itself was the product of conflict and was maintained by a yearly re-enactment of the struggle between "the forces making for activity and the forces making for inactivity."[19] The gods stood for the forces of activity, and chaos stood for rest and inactivity. Without the triumph of activity all life would cease to exist. Through this victory the earth would produce the necessary sustenance for man. Human society was the outcome of the ascendancy of the gods over the powers of darkness and disorder.

17. See, Georges Roux, *Ancient Iraq*, (Penguin Books, 1964), p. 11.
18. In ancient Mesopotamia, unlike in Egypt, the person of the king was not viewed as divine in himself; but his office was superhuman in origin, and the king held a mediatory rôle in the relationship between gods and men: see, Frankfort, *Kingship and the Gods*, pp. 224 & 237.
19. Thorkild Jacobsen, in, *Before Philosophy: The Intellectual Adventure of Ancient Man*, p. 187.

However, the Mesopotamian could never feel certain about his gods. After all, his gods possessed the same characteristics as himself. They, too, exhibited whatever qualities as well as defects that man himself retained.[20] He never imagined that his gods took any interest in man except for essentially selfish reasons. His most fundamental belief concerning the purpose of man was that he was created to live in unquestioning slavery to the gods. Specifically, he believed that "man was created to relieve the gods of toil"[21] and to serve their arbitrary needs. He further believed that the state existed, with the king at the top, to enforce subjection to the service of the gods.

Mesopotamian man submitted to this servitude as a necessary expedient for the protection that he in return, expected from the gods in the face of the threatening forces of chaos in nature. If he hoped to live the "good life," then such a cringing obedience to remote and unpredictable divinities was indispensable.[22] In his estimation success in life was connected to his status as slave of the gods. If he was a good slave, if he performed his duties well, then he might hope to receive some remittance, some favor, from his gods.[23] But of this he could never feel certain; and he definitely could not count on anything more than this. Much of his uncertainty was due to the utter indifference with which the gods looked upon man, and in part to the fact that the gods were themselves constantly threatened by an impending chaos. His gods were not omnipotent. This problem always weighs heavily upon men when they dissolve every distinction between the Creator and the creature.

The relationship of Mesopotamian man with his gods

20. "...highly intelligent, they could run out of ideas; generally righteous, they were also capable of evil thoughts and deeds; subject to love, hatred, anger, jealousy and all the other human passions, they ate and drank and got drunk; they quarrelled and fought and suffered and were wounded and could even die..." Roux, *Ancient Iraq*, p. 88.
21. Jacobsen, *Before Philosophy*, p. 88.
22. Jacobsen, *Before Philosophy*, p. 201.
23. Jacobsen, *Before Philosophy*, p. 220.

contained no moral component whatsoever. He felt no
sense of contrition or penitence towards the gods. The relationship was strictly *quid pro quo.* He might oscillate between
despair and exuberant happiness based upon how events
affected him, but he did not imagine that it was possible to
have intimate communion with his gods, nor did he ever feel
the slightest need that his gods should forgive his offenses.
"The Mesopotamians, while they knew themselves to be
subject to the decrees of the gods, had no reason to believe
that those decrees were necessarily just."[24]

In truth, we could say that Mesopotamian man venerated his gods because they establish the cosmic order and
the rhythm of nature in which man could feel secure, not
because his gods would avenge moral impurity. He did not
feel himself to be under the wrath of the gods for moral
offenses. Death, therefore, was not a curse for unrighteousness, but an ineluctable fate. It pertained to the nature of
man as man. Sometimes even the gods must suffer this fate,
though they do not experience its terrible permanence.
Mesopotamian man felt that at any time something could
happen to rob him of his happiness—for no apparent reason. This sense of fate produced in him a deep enervation
and forlorn hopelessness.

The Solomonic wisdom represented a radically different
outlook on life. It alone preserved the central Biblical truth
that God and man do not at all belong to the same cosmos
of experience, that God is indeed the Creator of all things,
and that man is His creature, fashioned in His image, for
the reasons mentioned in the last chapter. God is not under
a higher law of necessity as is man. No ultimate order or
chaos delimits God as well as man. God does not die, neither is He born, but He is from everlasting to everlasting.
Because God created all things, He is Lord and Sovereign
over all things. He determines the course of man's life.
Man's life is not at the mercy of some ultimate chance or
destiny. Death is the result of rebellion against God, not an

24. Frankfort, *Kingship and the Gods,* p. 278.

ineluctable fate. Man and God therefore stand in a moral relationship to one another, and the consequences of man's life are products of righteousness or unrighteousness. On the basis of covenant revelation man can know with certainty that his life is in the secure hand of his Lord and God, that he can count on prosperity for obedience, and misery and difficulty for disobedience./

Solomon's dedicatory prayer at the completion of the temple says it all. The opening words—"O Lord, God of Israel, there is no God like you in heaven above or on the earth below—you who keep your covenant of love with your servants who continue wholeheartedly in your way. You have kept your promise to your servant David my father; with your mouth you have promised and with your hand you have fulfilled it—as it is today." (I Kgs. 8:23,24)— express the foundational thought of the Solomonic wisdom. The remainder of the prayer unfolds a distinctly civilizational program for God's covenant people. The triumph of the Solomonic wisdom meant the triumph of the civilizational program for which it stood.

That this truth was fulfilled in the days of the historic Solomon appears clearly in I Kgs. 10:23—"King Solomon was greater in riches and wisdom than all the other kings of the earth. The whole world sought audience with Solomon to hear the wisdom God had put in his heart." One in particular came to hear Solomon's wisdom and to give gifts in testimony to the superiority of his civilization over her own. She was one of the great Pharaohs of Egypt itself, the Queen of Sheba.[25] In doing so, she recognized that it was to Solomon's God that credit should be given and to Whom in the last analysis all the honor and glory belonged.

25. I, for one, accept the opinion that the Queen of Sheba is Queen Hatshepsut of the famous XVIII dynasty, whose reign occurred not in the 15th cent. BC, but in the 10th cent. BC. For a discussion of this view and of the problem of dating the ancient chronology in general see: Immanuel Velikovsky, *Ages in Chaos: From the Exodus to King Akhnaton*, (New York: Doubleday & Company, Inc., 1952); and, Donovan A. Courville, *The Exodus Problem and its Ramifications, Vol. I*, (Loma Linda: Challenge Books, 1971).

III

The Wisdom of Christ

With the reign of king Solomon the Kingdom of God had truly reached the zenith of the splendor and dominion that God had purposed for its Old Testament form. What most confirms this is the way Solomon's wisdom manifestly surpassed the humanistic wisdom ideals found among the nations. The exaltation of Solomonic wisdom clearly displayed the preeminence of the Biblical wisdom and the incomparability of the God of which it spoke. It indicated that His word, and obedience to it alone, could provide the only foundation upon which culture and civilization might possibly be built. Anything else meant "vanity and chasing after wind!"

All the more extraordinary and perplexing is it when in I Kgs. 11 we abruptly discover that "as Solomon grew old, his wives turned his heart after other gods," that "his heart was not fully devoted to the Lord his God...." (v.4) Solomon, despite the pinnacle of grandeur to which God had elevated him, broke covenant with God and, in its place, substituted a false covenant with precisely those gods whose civilizational program Solomon had formerly proven to be vain, empty, and onerous in the extreme to their pious adherents. In his apostasy, Solomon brought down God's wrath not only upon himself but upon Israel as a whole. God would reduce Israel's prominence among the nations and cause her to learn the difference between servitude to Him and servitude to the false gods of the nations. She could expect that to forsake God would lead only to enslavement to God's enemies. The attitude of God's covenant head would redound to the benefit or curse of God's people.

It is natural that Solomon's unfaithfulness should excite in us the gravest astonishment. Did not Solomon, after all, possess every advantage? As was the case with Adam, whom he typified, Solomon was indeed granted every conceivable favor—wealth in abundance, peaceful conditions in which to enjoy it, and an unsurpassed understanding for the exercise of justice and righteous rule. What is more, God spoke directly to Solomon. He could not have mistaken the basis for his prosperity, and he would certainly have well understood what violation of the Lord's covenant involved. That despite all he knew and experienced in the way of God's favor he should nevertheless turn against the Lord and embrace abominable pagan practices and beliefs can only suggest that Solomon's rôle in the history of redemption was never intended to be permanent or final. While we do not lightly dismiss Solomon's sin and its consequence, it is clear that God had all along not meant that the historical Solomon should be the Man of Wisdom whom God would set everlastingly at the forefront of His Kingdom program. The humbling of the historical Solomon was necessary to clear the way for the Greater Solomon to take his rightful place at the head of God's covenant and at the center of His Kingdom. If human sinfulness in this instance accomplishes God's design it is only because God wishes us to understand that the redemption we need can be realized only through one who is himself without any stain or blemish. Not even Solomon, as glorious as he was, could guarantee that outcome; his sin proves this. We must look for one who is like Solomon, to be sure, but who cannot fail as he did.

Solomon's sin, while it does not invalidate the Solomonic wisdom, certainly points up its inadequacy. Those who would build up life on the basis of the Solomonic wisdom must be made to see its limitations. As long as God's redemptive program has not reached its culmination in

Jesus Christ, the wisdom which Solomon embodies remains, and must remain, incomplete. This realization must govern our view of the message of Ecclesiastes. The book's perspective is that of Solomon and therefore shares in its truth as well as its deficiency. And just as Solomon points ahead to Christ, so too must Ecclesiastes direct its readers. Indeed, we now have the advantage of seeing Ecclesiastes from the standpoint of Christ and so must grasp its lesson from his perspective and not solely from that of Solomon.

a. "Greater than Solomon"

In a stinging rebuke of the demand by the Pharisees and teachers of the law that he should perform some great miracle (Mt. 12:38), although on many occasions Jesus had done so in their very presence, in order that they might have an excuse to dismiss Jesus' Messianic pretensions, Jesus raised the comparison between Solomon and himself. Said he, "The Queen of the South will rise up at the judgment with this generation and condemn it; for she came from the ends of the earth to listen to Solomon's wisdom, and now a *greater than Solomon* is here." (Mt. 12:42)

Rather than to recite the possible reasons for the incident with the Pharisees and the teachers of the law which occasioned this comparison, our focus is simply to make known what Jesus himself thought of Solomon and the unique place which he conceived his wisdom to occupy. In Jesus' mind, Solomon was not just any example of a man of wisdom in the Old Testament, but was the quintessential man of wisdom. The comparison arises, then, to clarify the significance they each possess as designated bearer of God's word and therefore as proclaimer of His will. Both can rightly claim to have been specially appointed to address men with God's authority. However, Jesus indicates that his place in God's program supersedes that of Solomon. If a great queen in the ancient world travelled far to hear Solomon's words because they were from God, how much more ought the men of Jesus' day to listen and believe his words. Although Solomon was a wise man, and although the words he spoke were true and weighty, still what he said could not compare with what Jesus has to say. Neither could he do what Jesus does to demonstrate the power of his words. "Solomon with all his wisdom could not preach what Jesus preached, nor could he support his words with miraculous signs."[1] Despite the greatness of Solomon, he does not measure up to the Savior. On the other hand, neither is Solomon's rôle in the history of redemption negated. That is why Jesus can say to the teachers of the law that they will be condemned by one who came to hear Solomon's wisdom. Still it is their rejection of Christ that makes them accountable, a clear indication that they cannot claim to listen to Solomon when they refuse submission to Jesus' words. They themselves should recognize that Solomon was but a temporary substitute for Christ until the time he should come. Now that Christ has appeared, he is the true Solomon whom all men should hear and obey. Solomon is only great by reason of the greatness of Christ to whom he pointed.

Already at the birth of Jesus the superiority of the wisdom of God concerning him, over that of the nations who walk in darkness, is made to appear brilliantly. The comparison with the nations who came to hear Solomon is also evidently included. For in Matt. 2:1f we read of "Magi" or "wise men" from the East (i.e., from the civilization of Mesopotamia) who came to pay homage and honor and to render worship to the "king of the Jews." Even as king Solomon, who from the humanistic civilizations that dwelt apart from and opposed Israel attracted men to his wise counsel in tacit admission that his civilizational principles stood superior to their own, so too men from the East came to worship Jesus, whom they confess as a king and therefore as an eventual ruler of a civilizational program that will far

1. H.N. Ridderbos, *Matthew: The Bible Student's Commentary*, trans. by Ray Togtman, (Grand Rapids: Zondervan Publishing House, 1987), pp. 246,247.

exceed anything that man has ever been able even to imagine, let alone achieve, by his own perverse lights. Their tribute gives symbolic testimony to the bankruptcy of the humanistic ideals which issue from the religious goals of the kingdom of man and, at the same time, provides a prophetic foretaste of the triumph of the Kingdom of God to which the future is headed.

Ancient man longed for the appearance of God in human form. "For where," explains Stauffer, "the deity moves as a man among men, the dream of the ages is fulfilled, the pain of the world is scattered, and there is heaven on earth."[2] Through such a theophany man has continually hoped that the mystery of history will be cleared up and a permanent state of paradise on earth ushered in. With ancient man everywhere that desire was sought in "political form." As Stauffer further declares, "Again and again the hope of the nations is kindled by some promising ruler, and again and again this political eschatology is thwarted. But the disillusioned peoples recover, and raise once again the old advent cry. And every new advent proclamation is the renewal of the demand which in the end is to be fulfilled once for all—the longing for God to become man. That is the despairing repetition in the political advent hope of the classical world."[3] We saw this to be so in the underlying ideals of Egypt and Mesopotamia. Each looked to its king as the so-called savior promised. But just as Scripture proclaimed Solomon's wisdom worthier in excellence than that which was represented in those civilizations, even so the men of the East came to Christ and recognized the surpassing purpose of God in him. He is the only Messiah in whom the nations can legitimately place their hopes.

The restricted scope of the wisdom of Solomon would not seem as unequivocal as it does if we did not perceive the diminished importance of what his words say, or do not say,

2. Ethelbert Stauffer, *Christ and the Caesars*, trans. by K. and R. Gregor Smith, (Philadelphia: Westminster Press, 1955), p. 36.
3. Stauffer, *Christ and the Caesars*, p. 39.

concerning himself. By contrast, Christ's superiority over Solomon clearly appears by the astonishing claims Christ makes on his own behalf. We need merely to examine the sixth chapter of John. There Jesus repeatedly claims about himself what Solomon never could. For example, we read: "I am the bread of life. He who comes to me will never go hungry, and he who believes in me will never be thirsty." (v.35) Or, even more remarkable: "I tell you the truth, unless you eat the flesh of the Son of Man and drink his blood, you have no life in you. Whoever eats my flesh and drinks my blood has eternal life, and I will raise him up at the last day." (v.53f) Could Solomon, for all his wisdom, have ever uttered such a remark? Here, then, were words which in wisdom exceeded the wisdom of Solomon! When we recall that no *mere* man had ever had, or ever would have, wisdom greater than Solomon's, then we are bound to understand that the wisdom of Jesus is not that of a mere man, for Jesus is certainly more than man; he is the Epiphany of God himself. "No one has seen the father except the one who is from God...." (v.46) Consequently, Jesus can say, "The words I have spoken to you are Spirit and they are life." (v.63) Solomon's words might be a witness of life, but Jesus' words are life itself. The difference consists not in the truth which each speaks but in the ability that each has to make that truth effective against the corrosive consequences of sin. Solomon's wisdom lacked the *power* to make it efficacious for eternal life, and so genuine covenant life lacked its true ground. Peter's solemn confession sums up the transcending purpose of Jesus in redemptive history—"Lord, to whom shall we go? *You* have the words of eternal life." (v.68) All the wisdom of God must be seen to have its consummation in Christ who announced, "I am the resurrection and the life. He who believes in me will live, even though he dies; and whoever lives and believes in me will never die." (Jn. 11:25, 26) Clearly, Jesus connects Biblical wisdom to his own person in a way that Solomon could not. At the same time, he makes effective for the nations what Solomon could not

even hold onto with respect to himself. Rather than negate
the wisdom of Solomon, Jesus takes it up into his own person.

More than this, Jesus claims the indisputable right to dictate the terms of the civilizational program which that earlier Solomon by his wisdom had sought to promote. As
previously mentioned, Solomon's wisdom was not intended
to be solely for his private benefit, but was given to forge the
constructive basis of God's covenant and Kingdom. Having
a more than mere personal or pietistic application, the
Solomonic wisdom contained the necessary principles for a
thriving and prosperous civilization. We can say that its
grand design was to foster a complete Biblical culture and
total outlook on life for God's covenant people Israel. It is a
tragic misunderstanding of the present day, by so many in
the church, to think that Jesus has any less of a goal in mind.
Quite the contrary! We could even with perfect justice insist
that Jesus intends fully to realize the same civilizational
project that Solomon had earlier sought to accomplish, but
which, in fact, he could only foreshadow. In this respect,
Jesus does not introduce some "new" civilizational ideal
when he claims to replace the historical Solomon; rather he
expects to achieve that which God had purposed from the
outset. Indeed, he will totally succeed where the first
Solomon could only have been partially successful at best.

Perhaps no passage of Scripture manifests this truth
more than does the parable of the wise and foolish builder
in Matt. 7:24-27. Here Jesus makes crystal clear that his
word and obedience to it makes the basic difference
between the life-building activity that is wise and that which
is foolish. Hence, we read, "Therefore everyone who hears
these words of mine and puts them into practice is like a
wise man who built his house on the rock." (v.24) On the
other hand, "everyone who hears these words of mine and
does not put them into practice is like a foolish man who
built his house on sand." (v.26) For, says Jesus, a storm will
come—the storm of God's judgment on every man's

work—and every house (life) that is not firmly grounded will be utterly destroyed. "The rain came down, the streams rose, and the winds blew and beat against that house, and it fell with a great crash." (v.27)

All men seek to realize some form of civilization—that is what the house-building activity implies. The question is on what foundation do they build it? Man either builds in terms of the religious principles at the root of the kingdom of man, or he works on the firm foundation of the Kingdom of God. Jesus makes the response to his authoritative word the sole starting point for both.[4] Adherence to his word is the sole criterion determining who is truly wise. But more to the point, when Jesus makes obedience to his word the criterion, he does not mean that his word is now something different from what God had said earlier. Rather, he indicates that his word and God's word are one and the same. Obedience to the law of God is now seen to be obedience to Jesus and vice versa. Jesus does not negate God's law-word, but unites it with his own person. Jesus places himself and his word at the center of a complete civilizational program. Even the wisdom of Solomon must now be understood in the light of Jesus.

When we read farther on in the New Testament we discover the contrast Paul makes between "God's secret wisdom, a wisdom that has been hidden and that God destined for our glory before time began" (I Cor. 2:7) and what he styles the "wisdom of this age or of the rulers of this age, who are coming to nothing." (v.6) In Paul's mind, this latter wisdom—the humanistic wisdom—is really foolishness because it is a wisdom of death—"to those who are perishing...." (I Cor. 1:18) Yet, ironically, in the wisdom of those who are perishing it is the wisdom of God, founded on the cross of Christ, that is regarded to be foolish. In other words, a clear antithesis exists between the outlook of sinful man and the understanding that is freely given to those who have the mind of the Spirit. "The man without the Spirit

4. Ridderbos, *Matthew,* p. 155.

does not accept the things that come from the Spirit of God, for they are foolishness to him, and he cannot understand them, because they are Spiritually [i.e., by means of the Spirit] discerned." (2:14) Clearly, Paul means to imply that only two possible kinds of wisdom, matching two kinds of men, exists in the world: the wisdom of God in Christ "Christ Jesus, who has become for us wisdom from God" (1:30) and the so-called wisdom of would-be autonomous man who self-consciously despises the wisdom of God and desires only a wisdom that glorifies man. With the full manifestation of the "Wisdom of Christ" the opposition between the principles and values for which God's Kingdom stands and those of the kingdom of man comes more sharply into focus. It is necessary to stress this point for it bears on the way we read the book of Ecclesiastes.

Two thoughts about the humanistic wisdom that is spoken of in this portion of Scripture need emphasis. First, Paul mentions that the wisdom of this age is the wisdom of the "rulers" of this age, for the wisdom ideal that opposes Christ is civilizational in content. It is not just personal. "Rulers" has reference to all who seek to exercise power in any sense—but certainly in the political sense—in order to fashion a culture that will reflect the goals they believe in. They envisage as the product of the wisdom they champion a total civilizational structure. However, Paul does not mean to suggest that the wisdom of God, in contrast, represents no civilizational purpose. On the contrary! The point of his comparison is entirely to emphasize that the wisdom of God, by which He makes foolish the wisdom of the world, does indeed stand for the realization of a definite type of civilization. Second, Paul states that the wisdom ideal of the rulers of this age is historically that of the Greeks: "Greeks look for wisdom" (1:22). In the last chapter, we observed that the great civilizations of Egypt and Mesopotamia offered a humanistic wisdom program in contrast to that which Solomon advocated. We need to understand that, at the advent of Christ, the mantle of those ancient pagan wisdom viewpoints had been passed, says Paul, to the Greeks. Indeed, it is the Greeks who will place a greater man-centered accent upon the ideals which fallen man has endorsed from the time of his expulsion from the garden. At the same time, it is they who will give greater intellectual justification to the principles of the kingdom of man. Out of the humanistic ideals initiated by the Greeks man will grow in terms of his hostility towards God. That antagonism will take the form of an increasingly self-conscious opposition to Christ and his church. Since the time of Christ we can trace in the course of western history the outworking of the principles enunciated by the Greeks and see plainly that humanistic man to this day still rests his hope for civilization in terms of them.

b. The Greeks

Time and again we are told that our Western and European civilization was the product of the Greek genius. Upon their capacity for reflective and civilized modes of thought, so it is claimed, has our culture been built.[5] This avowal is not limited, however, to mere surface forms of thinking, but extends to the very heart of our culture's moral ideals and values. Their contribution, in other words, far from tangential, was determinative for every single feature of the civilization that our forefathers imagined and gave shape to, and which in turn has thoroughly molded our own outlook on life. In short, from the Greeks we supposedly have inherited all our ideas of right, wrong, good, evil, justice and truth. Bruno Snell did not hesitate to assert: "European thinking begins with the Greeks. They made it what it is: our only way of thinking; its authority, in the Western world, is undisputed...we use this thought...to focus upon...truth...with its help we hope to grasp the unchanging principles of this life."[6]

This is a sweeping assertion, one that is the product of

5. Thus, W.C.K. Guthrie, *The Greeks and Their Gods*, (Boston: Beacon Press, 1955), p. xll.

humanism's opposition to Christ and his Kingdom and that expresses the urgent longing to see realized the kingdom of man. This much is certainly true: it is the Greeks who have supplied the foundation for all that is humanistic in our Western culture. They have articulated the right, which disbelieving Esau relentlessly demanded, to possess the heritage of all that in truth belongs to believing Jacob. The offspring of the Greeks have passionately sought to dispossess the offspring of Christ. To the extent they have succeeded the result has been the substitution of a mess of pottage for true and lasting nourishment. What claims are made by and for the Greeks? Because wisdom is civilizational in nature, we must have some idea of what humanistic man in opposition to Christ has endeavored to construct for himself and his world. And because it was from the Greeks that our civilization took its humanistic starting point, we do well to understand something of what it was they believed.

The Greeks themselves derived many of their assumptions from the ancient pagan civilizations which preceded them. In the last chapter, we saw that the two most representative civilizations of the ancient pagan world were those of Egypt and Mesopotamia. These societies were strictly products of sinful and rebellious man's attempt to erect cultures in terms of ideals that deny the true and the living God and that glorify man. They were *Babel* cultures. Fundamental to their outlook on life was the effort to wipe out every distinction between Creator and creature. The dream of a culture and civilization on this basis had its origins in man's disobedience in the Garden of Eden, where man chose to heed Satan's claim that, instead of receiving curse and death from eating of the tree of the knowledge of good and evil, man would become "like God, knowing [i.e., determining] good and evil." (Gen. 3:5) The hope was to achieve, not lordship under God over all the earth, but an independent and autonomous god-like status over both himself and his

6. Bruno Snell, *The Discovery of the Mind*, (New York: Dover Publications, Inc., 1982), p. vl.

world. He would either bring God down to his level or raise himself to God's, but either way he would remove himself from ultimate responsibility for what God commands. He might accept advice from God, but he would not submit in unquestioning obedience to God's law-word. He refused to see that on submission or rebellion depended the issue of life or death.

It has been a futile endeavor. Instead of reducing God, God has reduced man to misery and death. Still, sin has taken powerful hold on the heart of man, and he remains obstinate in his rebellion. In spite of all that frustrates his efforts, he persists in his cherished desire for a world in which he alone is god over himself and all that he does. It is this ambition that continued to inspire the civilizational goals of ancient man throughout his history. If anything, this desire has only grown in strength with the passage of time. If Egypt and Mesopotamia possessed it, the Greeks represent a still greater outworking of its essential idea.

To begin, let us recall that at the very center of every difference between the civilization which set off Israel—as God intended her to be—from the civilizations around her was the irreconcilable antagonism between God and the gods. Israel was to have understood that every issue arising between her and her neighbors resolved itself into this basic opposition. This distinction they must ever uphold, God warned, and never attempt to eradicate. For ancient pagan man, his system of gods represented the heart of his covenant rebellion against God. Throughout the centuries this polytheistic culture was the shape assumed by his ideal of the kingdom of man—for the latter was the real ambition hidden behind the polytheistic religious facade. This is not to suggest that his gods were not real to him, that they were mere projections of his imagination. The opposite is indeed the case. Certainly, part of the reason for this is that, despite his rebellion, sinful man was incapable of completely effacing the sense of deity with which he had been creationally endowed. It long remained true, regardless of the perversion into which that sense of deity had degenerated. Man was created to depend upon God, and dissolving that feeling of dependence was not easy. Too, his experience was often one of grave uncertainty in the face of frequent disasters in the natural environment. He needed some compelling explanation to set his fears at rest. While man wanted to be his own god, there was too much in the world of his experience that eluded his control. Man was originally intended to live an ordered existence under God, but under conditions of curse disorder prevailed, and the cause of all real order appeared a mystery to him. It is this profoundly religious need to explain the principle of order in his world and experience that accounts for the existence and veneration of his gods. Without order, all would be chaos and destruction and a terror to man.

Still, as much as was possible, man wanted his gods on his terms. Consequently, his gods were not bigger than the order they were responsible for arranging. His gods might be stronger than man, but they were not absolute. Man groveled in his superstitious submission to them, yet his gods could not expect to have total authority over his life. They might establish the order of things, but they could not dispense with the order they created. His gods were finite. Man's real longing was to find some way in which his own rôle in the scheme of things could achieve the same indispensability as the gods'.

It is this breakthrough that was the accomplishment of the Greeks. Snell points to the real genius that was Greece: "Men gradually succeeded in depriving the gods of their power over the natural world and claiming it for themselves, for they had discovered that the human mind was itself divine."[7] It was this advance toward the goal of the kingdom of man that has been the reason for the paramount importance of the Greeks for humanistic man ever since. In the ancient world the issue had resolved itself into one between God and the gods, but the Greeks had succeeded

7. Snell, *The Discovery of the Mind,* p. 128.

in raising the matter to its truest proportions—that between God and man. By replacing god(s) with man the Greeks had finally realized the inner purpose of the kingdom of man. It is not surprising that secular men should so praise the Greeks as the true founders of Western civilization.

The "mind of man"—the "reason" in man—gradually acquired, certainly struggled to acquire, the exclusive status of "the arranger of order" in the Greek cultural outlook, a privilege previously reserved for the gods. The corollary to this revelation was the supposed original discovery of the realm of Nature and of "natural causation" by means of "definite and comprehensible laws."[8] One need not resort to the gods to find the reason for things; man had only to turn inward, and there he would realize that all that was necessary to understand his world lay within himself. The Greeks, it has been maintained, were the first to find the key to the liberation of man from his irrational dependence upon unknown and unknowable gods to whom he offered devotion out of sheer ignorance and superstitious fear. Again Snell: "...we have arrived at a rather general truth: primitive man feels that he is bound to the gods; he has not yet roused himself to an awareness of his own freedom. The Greeks were the first to break through this barrier, and thus founded our western civilization."[9]

This freedom, however, was not simply from the gods of ancient man in general, but from any Divinity whatever. In the final analysis, it was the claim of man to be free from the true and the living God. It meant the freedom to be man's *own* god. By emptying the world of gods, they filled it with Man. This bold declaration of independence led them to the belief that man was responsible for creating the ideal Man—that is, to fashion man and society in accordance with a vision of Man as the perfect standard and ultimate goal of all that was good and just. With this thought in

8. Werner Jaeger, *Paideia: The Ideals of Greek Culture*, Vol. I, (New York: Oxford University Press, 1945), p. xx.
9. Snell, *The Discovery of the Mind*, pp. 31,32.

mind, Jaeger is not mistaken when he observes with approval that "the man revealed in the work of the great Greeks is a political man."[10] The civilizational ideal of the Greeks was statist in nature and purpose. The state formed the highest good for man and all his cultural endeavors ought to serve that end. Wisdom for the Greeks meant that all men should further the interests of the state as the perfect goal of a justly ordered life. Outside and beyond this man could hope for nothing better. Is it surprising that the Greeks should have meant so much for humanistic man both then and now?

Greek culture and civilization formed a unified whole that took as its starting point the ideas expressed in their most famous poet, Homer. Voicing a commonplace in the field of classical studies, H.I. Marrou observed; "It is with Homer...that our history must begin. From him the Greek cultural tradition rises in an unbroken line...."[11] But more than just being the starting point, Homer represents the moral foundation on which the Greeks universally sought to build their civilizational ideal. Later thinkers may seek to modify his central viewpoint, but none ever contradicts him. He is the founding father of Greek culture. Through the lyric poets and the dramatists, through the early natural philosophers to their culmination in Plato and Aristotle, indeed, to the very conclusion of Greek cultural ideas in the Stoics and Epicureans, Homer's initial man-centered vision of life can be recognizably traced. Therefore, to apprehend correctly Greek culture with its humanistic goals requires, at the very least, some understanding of the Homeric founding contribution.

Homer's importance lies chiefly in two areas of thought: (1) his formation of the Olympian gods as cultural paradigms for human action, and (2) his elevation of the rôle of the "hero" to messianic status.

10. Jaeger, *Paideia*, p. xxv.
11. H.I. Marrou, *A History of Education in Antiquity*, trans. by George Lamb, (New York: A Mentor Book, 1964), p. 21.

On the one hand, Homer created an entirely new conception of the place and importance of the gods in the total scheme of things. Their purpose was no longer to explain the mystery of causality and order in the natural realm, but more importantly they function as the basis of order for human society and human purposes. His gods are culture-gods, not purely nature-gods. Their actions and behavior were meant to provide man with models for the creation of the *polis*—the city of man. While Homer retained the essential polytheistic perspective of ancient man in general, nevertheless he no longer believed that men existed to be slaves to the gods. Man has greater autonomy vis-a-vis the gods than ancient man would have expected. With Homer, "The human action (in the epic narrative) does not serve a higher, a divine cause, but quite the reverse: the story of the gods contains only so much as is needed to make the happenings on earth intelligible."[12] To some extent, man still feels dependent upon his gods, but overall the connection has become more that of admiration and emulation than of submission and abasement. Through Homer, man learned to look upon the order of the gods with lofty imitation instead of obsequious servility. His gods were venerated not because they were ethically superior to man—indeed, man was their equal in that respect—but because they were the Stronger Ones who could render favors and assist man in his desires for himself and his culture. In turn, the gods did not expect men to be good, only that they should render them their proper due.[13] The Olympians were conceived as lifting man above irrationalism and savage barbarism, enabling him to feel at home in the world. "Throughout his poems Homer has his gods appear in such manner that they do not force man down into the dust; on the contrary, when a god associates with a man, he elevates him, and makes him free, strong, courageous, certain of himself."[14] In Homer, one

12. Snell, *The Discovery of the Mind*, p. 37.
13. C.f., Walter Burkert, *Greek Religion, trans. by John Raffan*, (Cambridge: Harvard University Press, 1985).

senses, the gods are almost the boon companions of man. They certainly inspired man with dignity and pride; the gods led a robust existence, and man longed desperately to pattern himself on their model.

But however much Homeric man cherished the aristocratic society he enjoyed with his gods, he could never forget the great gap that yawned between them and himself. The gods were immortal, but man must surely die. This was not something decided by the gods, but simply happened to be the way things were. Indeed, men and gods were thought to spring from the same stock of existence, but destiny made one immortal and the other mortal. Still, man has long wanted to erase this distinction between himself and the gods and attain to divinity himself. Would it be possible to bridge the abyss that lay between them? Homer's contribution to this problem can be found in the second area of his importance—the conception of the hero-savior.

Homer, of course, did not invent the concept of the hero; it was an ideal that went back well into man's past. What he did was to offer the hero cult as a viable moral principle the practice of which offered a measure of immortality for otherwise luckless mortals. Though it might seem strange to call his knightly warriors savior-heroes, since so many of them perished on the plains of Ilion—the two greatest, Achilles and Hector, in particular—what they accomplished—fame and glory—manifests imperishable value. Even though they died, their noble example lives on for later generations to emulate. They offered the hope of lasting achievement, a type of salvation for human goals. Following Homer, the Greeks believed that by performing heroic deeds a man could achieve divinity and immortality.

The Homeric gods were immortal but limited. They were constrained in their activities as much by fate *(moira)* as was man. To speak of fate as governing the affairs of gods as well as men was the same as to say that *chance* ultimately decided every issue. Less and less in classical society do the

14. Snell, *The Discovery of the Mind*, p. 32.

Olympian gods stand for the hope of victory over chance and necessity, and more and more do the Greeks rest their confidence in the heroic ideal—the ideal of human virtue (*arete*).[15] Homer placed this hero quest at the center of an entire civilization's moral vision. It represents man's desire to exalt his own excellence. It is an ideal that gradually supersedes the rôle of the gods. For Homer, the hero model was the knightly warrior, but with the rise of philosophy the primary example of the heroic life became that of the philosopher and thinker, the precursor of "scientific" man who will figure so much in the modern era. The apex of this idea was reached with Plato's concept of the "philosopher-king," the chief man among men, the supreme moral authority for man's life in every respect. He represents the "expert" to whom all power and responsibility should be given for the realization of human societal aspirations. Through this idea of the hero in Greek thought the kingdom of man had attained a new level in its struggle against the kingdom of God.

Greek civilizational ideals—Homeric ones in particular—evolved into their final form in the period following the death of Alexander. This, the Hellenistic period, was the time when Greek values were everywhere predominant. It was also the time when the Stoics and the Epicureans, those final inheritors of Homer, held undisputed sway with the educated and the cultural elites. At this stage, the gods had receded well into the background, and in their place emerged the "cult of chance." The ancients and Homer had sought to delimit the gods by fate. Now, chance or fortune (*tyche, fortuna*) had arisen preeminent. No longer was there any need felt for personal gods to explain the principle of order in man's world. For the Stoics especially, "Fate was the power that kept order in the world."[16] Here we encounter the beginnings of the concept of "natural law" that will

15. Charles Norris Cochrane, *Christianity and Classical Culture*, (New York: Oxford University Press, 1957), pp. 419 & 443.
16. G.J. Withrow, *Time in History*, (New York: Oxford University Press, 1989), p. 48.

loom so large in the moral estimation of humanistic man in the West. It will prove to be his primary weapon in the war against God and Christ.

From the Stoics emerged a moral vision of life founded upon a completely impersonal universe. Still, all was not lost; there remained human virtue *(virtus)*, the only hope which man possesses of living wisely in the face of capricious destiny. If fate stood for the final arbiter of the world, the goal of life should be to choose to live in terms with it. Man's highest purpose should be the achievement of *ataraxia*, "peace of mind," so that he may not be buffeted by what fate dispenses. The means to attain this goal was *apathiea*— the total absence of all feelings and disturbing passions which arise from the body and material things. It was a man's duty to deprive himself of all that agitated his senses and to give himself solely to the things of the mind. Here alone he could find salvation and happiness. This Stoic doctrine formed the basis of the "religion of culture," so very characteristic of Hellenistic man. To be "learned" meant immortality and divinity.

We may well understand why Paul referred to the Greeks as those who "seek after wisdom." The whole of Greek ideals, from Homer to the Stoics, represented man's attempt at self-salvation and the glorification of man. Undoubtedly they would have viewed the cross of Christ as foolishness, for in their vaunted estimation it stood not for man's exaltation but for his debasement to a foul barbarian superstition. They would see it as the denigration of man and an enervation of any civilizational effort.

The message of Ecclesiastes is far removed from any notion of Stoical fatalism. Its central concern is persistently to emphasize that it is not fate but the God of the covenant who rules the affairs of men. Men who have endeavored to explain the principle of order and purpose as the product of chance have not learned *to reckon with the God* in Whom alone man can expect to find the basis of his life, both now and forever.

Part II
The Text

IV

Prologue: The Root of the Problem
1:1-11

Among modern commentators on the Book of Ecclesiastes, scarcely one has understood the Biblical covenant framework of its meaning. Nearly all have regarded its thoughts to be merely the personal ruminations of one man on the logic of the "human situation as such." If anything, his thinking is portrayed as the inescapably pessimistic conclusion of one compelled to observe that man's life is circumscribed by an unexplainable necessity, that the circumstances that attend common human experience ultimately rest upon the enigmatic will of a *Deus Absconditus*, a hidden god who refuses to permit man any knowledge of the meaning of his life and the reasons for events, and who arbitrarily burdens him with mortality and finitude. If anything positive is to be found in the book it is cancelled out by the negative reflections which pervade it. What is said concerns all men in general—man as a mere human being and nothing more. No distinction is recognized to exist between "covenant keepers" and "covenant breakers"; between the righteous and the wicked; between God's kingdom and people and the kingdom of man. The author's thoughts about men lack any conception of a fundamental "religious" difference between them. In his humble opinion (he does not speak "dogmatically") man is left to make the best of his situation, and in the end he must succumb to the ultimate meaninglessness of his existence and circumstances. The book proffers no lasting hope, no firm foundation on which to build life and face the future, neither for the near term nor in the final sense. If any "gospel" is to be hoped for, it must be found only by abandoning the book altogether and (if one has any Christian sensibility at all) turning to the sweet words of Jesus as we find them in the New Testament. A pious trust in Jesus can alone save us from the burden of meaninglessness and vanity that is inescapably ours in this life. Still, trusting Jesus does not remove the problem: it merely enables one to retain some sort of emotional solace in spite of it.

To the majority of commentators Ecclesiastes is not "words of God"; it is a purely human composition, not to any conspicuous degree dissimilar from those found in the ancient world generally. The most persistent feature in the over-all interpretation of the book is the steadfast avoidance of any mention of "sin" as the root cause of man's problem. And here we do not have in mind "personal moral failings," which would readily be acceptable; rather, we mean Adam's covenant transgression in the Garden which was responsible for the corruption and rebellion of the race as a whole. Further, no mention is even remotely made of God's righteous judgment on such willful disobedience, nor of His establishment of a Covenant of Redemption carrying the promise of complete deliverance from the curse and its consequences. What is more, it would be held, the author of Ecclesiastes had no such thoughts in mind. Instead, as far as he was concerned, the problem of man's life lies simply in his finitude. It is man's existence as a creature, not as a sinner, that calls forth the declaration of futility and meaninglessness. As one recent commentator asserts: "Man's mind is by its very nature finite...his creator has deliberately denied to him...the capability of discovering any principle which will explain why things happen as they do...this *ignorance* [my emphasis] is one of the basic causes of human frustration in general."[1]

The chief cause of man's problem, then, is the ignorance

1. R.N. Whybray, *Ecclesiastes: The New Century Bible Commentary*, (Grand Rapids: Wm. B. Eerdman's Publ. Co., 1989), p. 26.

which encloses him and for which, we may note, he is not responsible. God is to be blamed, for He created man to live in frustration in the first place. He refused to allow man any knowledge as to the why of things. Whybray cannot admit that the message of Ecclesiastes should be studied in the light of Scripture as a whole. The unity of God's word forms no part of his interpretation. Consequently, he takes the words of the author of the book at their face value. No mention can be made of God's curse on man as a punishment for his rebellion. As with humanist thinkers in general, he can only say that it is because man is *less than God* that his life is subjected to inevitable vanity and meaninglessness.

Even as reliable a Biblical expositor as H.C. Leupold, who at least accepted the God-inspired authorship of the book, could find no content to its message other than to say that its purpose was "to persuade men not to have undue confidence in worldly treasures."[2] What man should have confidence in he is reluctant to say. At most, life is such that, in order to get on as best one can, man must resign himself to God's mysterious ways. To do so demands certain negative requirements, namely, the avoidance of all "formalism, discontent, attempting to solve what lies beyond our ken...and the like."[3] The purpose of the book is to remind man that he is a mere creature whose life is a haphazard affair at best and an unrelieved tension at worst. If he is buffeted about, man can rest assured that it is God who does the buffeting, but more than this he cannot and need not know.

A third commentator sees a slightly different purpose in the book. It was intended to counter man's high pretensions of himself and his wisdom; it was an attack upon man's hubris—just as the Greek gods responding, when men lost the true sense of their place in the scheme of things, acted with vengeance to cut man once again down to size and to

2. H.C. Leupold, *Exposition of Ecclesiastes*, (Grand Rapids: Baker Book House, 1952), pp. 19f.
3. Leupold, *Exposition of Ecclesiastes*, p.18.

remind him that mortality was his eternal lot. Hence, the book serves to remind man that, whatever knowledge he may possibly possess, it can never claim to be a "self-sufficient system."[4] One may never pretend to speak anything with certainty and conviction. Man must never claim to have the final answer to life's riddle. Most especially he must never assume that he can say anything definite about God and His ways, for "God and his actions are never the prisoners of fixed patterns...." God will always elude our attempts to understand Him. Apparently, He has never spoken a clear word of revelation that man can believe and know with real confidence. No final interpretation of God and His will is afforded man, who must remain open to new vistas and insights. We are fated to be constantly pursuing knowledge but never finally having it. Ecclesiastes represents a protest against all closed systems of truth; it opposes man in his attempts to know beyond what he is permitted. No man, no group—not even the church—has all the answers. Mankind possesses many voices, and together they can provide a partial insight at best. The voice of the covenant keeper has no advantage over that of the covenant breaker. What Ecclesiastes teaches us is that life ultimately has no clear explanation; it merely exhibits observable tendencies and allows for useful temporary perspectives.

We, for our part, shall insist that the Preacher's[5] words are grounded in the covenant, that he means to speak from the standpoint of the Solomonic[6] wisdom, which is the Bib-

---

4. J.A. Loader, *Ecclesiastes,* trans. by John Vriend, (Grand Rapids: William B. Eerdmans Publishing Company, 1986), p. 14.
5. "Preacher" translates the word Qoheleth. An acceptable alternative reading would be "Teacher," for the writer is not a preacher in our sense of the term.
6. The author of the book is not Solomon, nor was the book written in the time of Solomon: it is post-exilic. For a discussion of authorship and dating of the book see the introductory comments by Whybray and Loader. However, while Solomon did not author the book, it is nevertheless "Solomonic" in content. This further implies that in the ultimate sense it is Christ who is the speaker in the book.

lical standpoint in its entirety as he understood it. It is his purpose to announce this thought in 1:1. Commentators wish to explain this first verse as the addition of a later editor. They do so out of sheer speculation. It is possible to maintain this viewpoint so long as one does not accept that Ecclesiastes has any basic biblical message to it. But 1:1 is the announcement of the Preacher's perspective, the standpoint from which all his thoughts will be addressed. It is his claim to speak as a God-inspired disciple of Solomon, much the same as Paul was an inspired disciple of Christ. It is to say that all that follows is framed by the covenant Solomonic perspective which we outlined in Part I. Consequently, all that is contained in that perspective will either be explicitly stated or implied throughout. This includes the promise to Abraham, the laws of Moses, and everything that pertains to the difference between Israel and the nations. Above all, it will mean that the Preacher views sin and its consequences to be the *root of the problem*, not the fact that man is finite. This most basic problem of man involves the creation in its totality. Man must be made to see that a solution to his problem must involve the total renewal of the creation. Man lives under a curse which affects his life in every sense. When the Preacher claims to speak as a disciple of Solomon he is saying that the answer lies in God's redemptive program. Apart from this all man's life is vanity and meaninglessness.

In speaking from the Solomonic standpoint the Preacher insists that, first, the fundamental problem of man's life cannot be removed by the power of man himself. This is the purpose of the negative tone of his message. He wishes to drive home man's total inability to deliver himself from the heavy burden under which he lives. It is an assault on all the wisdom ideals of humanistic man; that is, man in his self-proclaimed autonomy from the true and the living God. By stressing the vanity of all things, he teaches that it is in the God of the covenant alone that the solution to man's problem must be found, that the pagan ideals man believes in

are without the slightest effect in changing his situation. It is
vain to look to man. Second, man's problem is not merely
personal, but it is creational in scope. Therefore, the solution to his problem must involve a total renewal of the creation. Third, his message contains a complete civilizational
program. The deliverance that man needs must set him on
a new course of life *in* God's creation, one that is to be
directed by God's law (12:13). At no point does the book
offer escape from God's creation, and God's purpose for
man in it, as the answer to man's problem.

In 1:2 the proclamation of man's problem is loudly her-
alded, for undoubtedly the Preacher intends to stress here
and throughout the book the centrality of this, man's most
fundamental problem. Nothing can compare with it; nothing ranks along side it as man's chief concern. When, therefore, he sharply exclaims, "Utterly meaningless! Everything
is meaningless" the Preacher has in mind the condition of
man as it now exists, not because man is finite but because
he is fallen. His thoughts are neither the product of philo-
sophical reflections nor of nihilistic despair. He knows the
reason for the meaninglessness (or vanity) that imposes
upon man's life and experience: it is the curse of God. Consequently, the situation in which man now finds himself is
not the result of the impersonal actions of nature, but of the
personal actions of God against him. It is the result of judgment, not natural development.

Because this pronouncement is made with such unre-
strained vehemence it is thought by some to constitute the
theme of the book. But by itself it forms a mere sub-theme
at best. It must be combined with the latter half of 1:13 to
make any sense at all. Only then does it enter into the central idea of the book, which we will touch on in the next
chapter. In the meantime, it must be clearly understood
that, while the Preacher's remarks focus on the most basic
issue which concerns man, he parts company with all views
that hold that man's present condition in the world is altogether normal. His entire purpose is to emphasize that

man's life hinges above all else on his relationship to his Creator and Redeemer. Moreover, the use of the superlative ("Utterly meaningless") is meant to underscore the idea that no area of man's life, no aspect of his existence, escapes from the burden under which he lives. It is a comprehensive problem, and it requires a comprehensive solution.

If the Preacher did not emphatically state that it was the curse that accounts for the meaninglessness of everything, it was because he took for granted that his audience would have understood this. For while he speaks of the situation of all men in general, and directs his thoughts at the self-confidence of humanistic man specifically, nevertheless his comments are addressed to the covenant sons of Israel. His words were spoken at a time when great temptation was being offered to God's people to abandon the covenant and adopt the ideals and practices of the world. His purpose is to remind his listeners that to stray from the covenant is to invite the crushing burden of the curse upon them without any hope—which has become the lot of the covenant breaker. At this juncture of redemptive history the true Israel had been reduced in significance next to the cultures which surrounded her. She might think that God's covenant with her no longer mattered. The nations believed in Man. Israel must remember that it is God with Whom we have to do.

1:3 draws attention to the real concern of the Preacher arising out of the curse and the problem of its consequences. It has to do with man, not man as simply an ordinary creature in the world, but man in terms of his creation in God's image and his exalted calling to have dominion under God. The Preacher understands perfectly man's intended place in the creation. He knows full well that man was created and equipped to be God's special servant and companion in the task of building God's kingdom and of transforming the earth so that its features would permanently resemble the glory of God. "Under the sun" refers both to the location where God placed man to dwell and the extent of the realm

he was intended to transform on God's behalf. By implication it also points to the place where the curse of God does
its greatest damage. Man was created to "work," to labor;
his work was expected to achieve *everlasting* results. Now, on
account of sin, all his labor can achieve no lasting product.
His every effort eventually decays. He does not receive the
remaining fruits of his labor. In time, death intervenes to
remove him from "under the sun" altogether. Man possesses
no resources within himself to remedy this basic fact about
himself and his activity in the world.

The Preacher is not talking simply about "making a living." The labor he has in mind was the work of achieving
eternal life and rest which God originally gave to Adam to
accomplish. The thought is that man is doomed to failure in
that effort unless God should intervene on his behalf and, by
the power of His grace, enable man to achieve what he
could not even hope to do otherwise. Little do we realize
that man's efforts throughout history at building cultures
and civilizations have been suffused with the religious goal
of achieving eternal life. The Preacher warns us that all such
endeavors by man are unattainable so long as he fails to
comes to grips with the root of his problem. Man believes
implicitly that nature (i.e., creation) is pliable to his wishes.
The Preacher says that God's curse is more powerful than
nature. It is a negative indication that man's hope lies solely
in the power of God. It is the Preacher's way of breaking
with all cosmic religious outlooks and asserting that God
and nature are not to be identified with one another.

In verses 4-11 the Preacher directs our thoughts to the
realms of nature and history as the arena of man's experience. Both are symbolic reminders that man's activity does
not attain to a permanent result, but is caught in a cycle of
repetition and futility. Verses 4-7 especially teach a powerful
lesson from nature. A generation comes and a generation
goes; the sun rises and the sun sets; the wind blows from one
direction, then another; the waters flow to the sea, but the
sea is never filled up, but it gives up its water to the atmo-

sphere only to begin the process again. All these activities are events over which man has no control. He is reminded that his own life is not in his power. The realm of nature does not bend to his wish to create something of truly enduring value. All that continues is a ceaseless repetition. He cannot look to nature to discover eternal life.

Finally, in verses 8-11 the Preacher reflects on the world of mankind in particular; for his main concern is how the curse of God affects, as we said, the labors of man. These verses point out a troubling paradox; man continues to labor and to hope for permanent results from his endeavors, yet he fails either to recognize or admit that all his efforts are, like nature, caught in an endless cycle. In spite of all his exertions, man never really gets anywhere, but repeatedly makes the same attempt to do so. 1:8 especially indicates the confidence which men resolutely maintain regarding their ideals and goals for culture and civilization. Loader is undoubtedly correct to translate this verse not "all *things* are wearisome," but "all *words* are full of labor."[7] This reminds us that the Preacher, as a disciple of Solomonic wisdom, intends to point up the futility of humanistic wisdom. Men refuse to reckon with God and His actions, and so they continue to believe that they are in possession of a true explanation of life and its purpose. Their "words" constantly spew forth to direct and guide men in the achievement of the truly good life. Nowhere does man labor with greater energy than in the promotion of his values and his vision for the perfect society. His eyes and ears are always engaged in the quest to learn with the expectation that he will unlock the secret of breaking through the cycle of nature and time and be able to realize a permanent and everlasting condition for mankind as a whole. This goal of humanistic man has ever remained the same. There is nothing really "new" in this respect.

When, therefore, the Preacher rhetorically asks in 1:10 if

---

7. Loader, *Ecclesiastes*, pp. 21,22.

anything that man does is "new" (i.e., permanent), he means to say that history demonstrates otherwise. He concludes that men do not truly learn from history as God meant that they should. Men persistently fail to recognize that the wisdom ideals of the present were the same as those of the past. They accomplished nothing then, nor will they do so now. Men simply choose to disregard this fact, as he indicates in 1:11. Moreover, the future will be no different. Ancient man believed that history could be dispensed with altogether, for he did not want to reckon with change. It was a reminder to him of his own transience. Man has long wanted to arrest history in order to usher in a final state of things. The real problem is that he does not wish to reckon with the God of history.

In these opening verses which we have styled the *Prologue*, the Preacher sets the tone for all that he intends to say hereafter. The mood is somber but not one of despair. If his thoughts appear negative it is only because he wishes to draw attention to the positive message that he will also convey. In nature and in the human world man cannot find anything that will rescue him and his endeavors from the burden under which his sin has placed him. He must be confronted with the total futility of his wisdom ideals if he is to discover any "words" of wisdom that will lead to life everlasting. In the God of the covenant is to be found the deliverance from "Utterly meaningless!"

V

The Powerlessness of the Wise
1:12–3:15

At 1:12 the Preacher begins the exposition of the ideas which will form the main contours of his book.[1] As he does so, he feels the need once again to stress the covenant Solomonic perspective upon which his thinking is based. When he muses on the nature of human experience "under the sun," it is as a child of the covenant that he makes his evaluations. Accordingly, his prognoses are framed by the word-revelation that stands at the center of God's covenant; he does not speak merely as his experience and reflection dictate. Because his viewpoint is Solomonic, his thoughts are preeminently God's explanation of man's experience, so that he does not begin with the notion that his experience is sufficient unto itself to illumine his understanding and to provide direction and insight.

Still, his procedure is not merely to quote from God's covenant word; rather he explains man's experience in the world out of a deepened insight from it. God meant that, by means of concentrated study and intellectual reflection, man should seek to understand the world of his experience; by doing so he should gain a cumulative insight of it and so increase in the ability to exercise dominion over it. His knowledge would enhance the *powers* of responsible lordship. This connection between wisdom, knowledge, understand-

1. The chapter-headings that start here were borrowed, with some modification, from the outline provided by E. Th. Van Den Born in his helpful little work *De Wijsheid van den Prediker,* (Kampen, The Netherlands: J.H. Kok, 1939).

ing and power we endeavored to clarify earlier. God's intent
was that His word should stand at the center of that enterprise. No aspect of the creation which God had legitimately
subjected to the labors of man could be left out of account.
It is with this in mind that the Preacher declares in 1:13: "I
devoted myself to study and to explore by wisdom *all* that is
done under heaven." His comment refers principally to man
as God's dominion servant and the scope of the task that
God had given to him. Our attention is drawn to the original Adamic calling, and by taking his direction from it the
Preacher emphasizes that its restoration thus far in redemptive history had found its greatest realization in Solomon
and in the wisdom (civilizational) program for which he
stood. It further implies that man, the more successfully to
exercise dominion, ought to acquire a comprehensive
insight into the unity of all his experience under God. Just as
God's knowledge of His work is completely integrated, so
too, in a finite sense, should man's be. Man's attempt to
build life was not meant to achieve living for its own sake
but to form a kingdom. Every facet of life should be bound
together.

In our age Christians have lost sight of the integrated
nature of life under God as originally intended. For many, a
dualistic outlook predominates. The perverse tendency is to
compartmentalize life into a realm of *nature* on the one hand
and a realm of *grace* on the other. In the former, Christians
proceed on the assumption that life should generally be
ordered by a knowledge and understanding of man that
need not essentially be controlled by Scripture, while the latter is politely reserved for those things regarded as belonging to God, an area that in our day has been virtually
reduced to personal and subjective interests. This has left
the door open for pagan ideals to become the governing
principles for great areas of the Church's life in the world,
especially in society. Restricting God's word to a mere portion of the Christian man's experience has profoundly distorted the total claim of covenant responsibility for *all* that is

done "under heaven." But as J. Gresham Machen wisely remarked, "...the field of Christianity is the world. The Christian cannot be satisfied so long as any human activity is either opposed to Christianity or out of all connection with Christianity. The Christian...cannot be indifferent to any branch of earnest human endeavor. *It must all be brought into some relation* to the gospel."[2] It is precisely this perspective that governs the thinking of the Preacher in his approach to wisdom. He is supremely aware that true Biblical wisdom applies to *all* aspects of man's experience. The understanding of man's life must be total and comprehensive. No area of man's life can be left out of his relation to God and the covenant.

It is for this reason that he immediately adds the forceful words of the latter part of verse 13, that relate to what he has said in the first part of the verse. "What a heavy burden God has laid on men!" To understand clearly the Preacher's intensions here requires careful thought. For when he registers his mind with such emphatic certainty and conviction it is not at all because he has just reached the despairing end of a bitter "investigation by wisdom." Quite the contrary! Far from drawing some dejected conclusion with the utterance of these words, he rather vociferously announces his premise! They are words which do not form the outcome of his thinking, instead they stand altogether at the outset and shape for every essential the direction his thought, disciplined by covenant Solomonic wisdom, must take. As a man who speaks within the framework of covenant wisdom he is supremely aware that his words must have a God-centered foundation if they are to claim any validity. He knows that it is with God Whom all men have to do and clearly realizes that his study of wisdom must reckon with Him at the beginning and in all stages of his endeavor and not merely at the end. That is why he makes this assertion at the very

2. J. Gresham Machen, Education, *Christianity, and the State,* ed. John W. Robbins, (Jefferson, Maryland: The Trinity Foundation, 1987), p. 50. (emphasis mine)

beginning of the book and not at the conclusion. Interpreters who refuse to see any systematic logic in the book do well to consider this fact.

For example, we cannot agree with Whybray's claim that Ecclesiastes is "not a single systematic treatise in which there is a progression from a set of premisses to a logical conclusion."[3] The Preacher's whole purpose in acknowledging God from the outset is precisely to make the "progression" of his thought clear. He indicates that the problem of the vanity and meaninglessness of things is tied up with man's profoundly disturbed relationship to God. The burden of God is a burden imposed *by* God for a discernible reason. It is meant to challenge man's self-proclaimed autonomy from God and from responsibility to God's covenant word. The remainder of the book clearly unfolds the *logical* implications of this confrontation between man and God, however much some may wish to deny its *systematic* nature.

With these words—"What a heavy burden God has laid on men!"—the Preacher proclaims the real theme that runs through the book with relentless persistence. Each major section of the book, which forms a chapter of our own study, shows this theme returning again and again in order to underscore God's absolute predominance over the life of man. It is this fact with which humanistic man in his wisdom does not wish to reckon, but which the book will make plain that he must. Man in his rebellion would dispense with God. The Preacher's purpose is to make clear that man's life in the world is without any foundation if he refuses to reckon above all with God. Because man stands under God's curse he must be made to take account of the fact that it is God Who is both the cause of the condition that troubles his life as well as the solution to it. Wisdom, if it is to be of ultimate use to man, must begin where the Preacher declares that he must begin—with God and with what God does.

3. Whybray, *Ecclesiastes*, p. 19.

Having declared his starting-point, the Preacher, in verses 14–18 makes a broad comment on the profitability of wisdom. He directs his observations at the man who claims to be wise, for the root problem lies in man; wisdom in man is affected by the nature of man. His remarks are directed primarily at humanistic wisdom, the wisdom of man in rebellion against God, and the fact that his wisdom is completely *powerless* to deliver on the ideals for which it speaks. The grand claims of humanistic man totally disregard the moral and religious corruption that is at the center of his being. There is a depravity in man's nature that his wisdom cannot resolve, and that also distorts his apprehension of true wisdom. "What is twisted cannot be straightened; what is lacking cannot be counted." (v.15) Until this problem is dealt with man will continue to live under a false wisdom, and his endeavors will reflect the vanity of doing so.

However, when we take a closer look in particular at vv. 16–18, we see another dimension to the Preacher's thought that also flows through the book. His placing the accent upon his own wisdom pursuit indicates that he not only has something to say concerning the wisdom of men outside the covenant, but that he intends to clarify a problem for Solomonic wisdom as well. Specifically, it, too, exhibits a certain powerlessness. Although Solomon in his wisdom understood the root of man's problem, he was unable fundamentally to do anything about it. This is the thought the Preacher expresses in v. 18: "For with much wisdom comes much sorrow, the more knowledge, the more grief." It is not that his wisdom is useless, it is only that it is impotent to rectify the crookedness at the center of man's being and experience. Thus, in the Preacher's analogy, wisdom may as well seek to capture the wind. It is an indication that man's problem is deep-seated and intractable for man. If this was true from Solomon's viewpoint within the covenant, how much more so from that of man outside the covenant! The point is not to detract from Solomon, nor to claim that his wisdom is no better than the humanistic wisdom outside of Israel;

rather, it is to show that Solomon must pale before Christ in whom there will not only be found the wisdom men need, but also the power to make it efficacious in the lives of God's people. Wisdom—even Solomon's—is of no value if it cannot permanently correct the sinfulness of man. Still, the Solomonic wisdom remains sufficient to address the true nature of man's problem and to direct him to the God with Whom he must reckon if he hopes to find deliverance from vanity and meaninglessness. If men would heed Solomon, they will be compelled to hope in Christ.

Chapter 2:1–11 continues the series of reflections on the nature of the problem of wisdom and life. The Preacher here has in mind wisdom in its departure from the covenant. The question arises, since wisdom is powerless to straighten what is crooked, how does this affect the enjoyment of life and the accumulation of life's treasures? Can wisdom find some way to heal the sorrow and pain which seems to be its only reward? Is it possible to find some means in the realm of man's experience to divert attention from the anguish it knows? Can wisdom escape the hurt and continue to speak with wisdom? The reader will need to be aware that in the context of these verses the "experiment of wisdom" with life's amusements and labors to acquire possessions and pleasures is attempted "without God in mind,"[4] so that, strictly speaking, it is not a reference to Solomon's own life. The thought here is what the humanist wise recommend—that man can escape from his problem and not have to confront it.

These verses do not imply, as Loader maintains, that the Preacher has turned to the lifestyle of the fool.[5] There are two reasons to resist this suggestion: one is that twice, in v. 3 and again in v. 9, the Preacher emphasizes that his investigation into this matter is done with wisdom guiding him. This would hardly be expected of the fool. Second, if he had adopted the lifestyle of the fool he would have had an

4. Leupold, *Ecclesiastes*, p. 61.
5. Leupold, *Ecclesiastes*, p. 29.

answer to the fool's problem, namely he ought to abandon that lifestyle and accept the ways of wisdom; but this he emphatically does not say. For the problem at this point concerns something in the nature of wisdom alone and does not yet address the matter of foolishness. Consequently, the pleasures and cultural labors he refers to are entirely legitimate ones in God's world. He does not condemn this activity. His point is to claim that the wise man cannot find in them a diversion from his sorrow. He does not deny that some reward can be found in these pursuits (v.10), but he recognizes that ultimately that reward is negated by the continuation of man's basic problem. Of what value then is such labor? It, too, is a chasing after the wind. In these activities, however beneficial, no rest for the soul is to be found. And by the sheer absence of God in this activity he lays his finger once again on the presumptions of humanistic man.

In this context (of verses 1:12–3:15) the Preacher takes his overriding concern, the *powerlessness of the wise*, through a series of reflections on the problem towards an intended conclusion. Each group of sub-verses along the route pushes the issue relentlessly in the direction he wishes it to go. These groupings of his thought are not unrelated, but are designed to examine the humanist's dilemma from a select number of crucial angles. He means to assault the major props on which man seeks to rest his self-declared autonomy from God. His purpose is to leave no escape for secular man except to take account of the God of the covenant.

Thus, in 2:12–16 he takes the matter one step further. Now from a direct comparison of the wise man with the fool he purposes to highlight the question of the advantage of having wisdom. Even so, let us carefully note that the comparison is not so much between wisdom and foolishness as such as it is between the wise *man* and the fool, for the core of the problem lies in man. He may perfectly agree that, as characteristics taken by themselves, wisdom stands superior to foolishness. He says as much in vv. 13 & 14: "I saw that

wisdom is better than folly, just as light is better than darkness," etc. He has, of course, principally in mind the covenant wisdom as that which is truly light. However, if
wisdom—and here the problem refers most especially to
man apart from God—does not have the *power* to deliver
from death the man who claims to have it, then what possible advantage is his wisdom? In truth, the supposedly wise
man must experience the same consequences of sin as the
fool. Why, then, go to the trouble to acquire wisdom? Does
this mean that, far as the Preacher is concerned, it makes no
difference whether men are wise or fools? Not at all! The
Preacher does not stand here for some sort of values relativ-
ism. He looks at matters as they must add up for men in
their rebellion against God. For, once more, the absence of
the mention of God in the context suggests that that is what
he means to imply. By taking the issue to its ultimate—
death—he has brought the matter of wisdom to the only
conclusion to which it can possibly arrive unless man reck-
ons with the God of the covenant. Only thus can he hope to
find the answer to the powerlessness of the wise as well as to
justify wisdom over foolishness.

     In the next set of verses, 17–23, the Preacher has at last
arrived at the summation of his thought concerning man in
his rebellion against God and what this means for his life
and ideals. All that remains is to "hate life" (vv. 17f). Because
secular man cannot reckon with his sin and rebellion he
finds that life must turn out to be a bitter disappointment.
When man has believed so supremely in man and his life
becomes intolerable because his goal of being his own god
has failed to accomplish the perfect life that he expected, his
response inevitably becomes one of nihilism and complete
despair of all his cherished values. His only option is totally
to hate himself and all of life; his lone goal is to reduce all to
disorder in the vain hope that somehow a new order will
emerge. All man's attempts to fashion a world for himself in
opposition to God are bound to lead to futility and frustration. In the end he loses patience, for as Rushdoony has

observed, "even as patience is associated with hope, so by implication the loss of hope means impatience. When we have no hope, both waiting and tribulations become meaningless to us, and we cannot then patiently endure them."[6] The Preacher expresses the bitterness that must result when one considers that man's efforts are transitory. For man must die and leave the fruits of his labors to the next generation, and he cannot guarantee that it will continue his ideals or revert to foolishness.

Having described the human condition at its nadir, man in his self-proclaimed independence from God, the Preacher introduces a transition passage that leads to the culmination of his thought in this section. Calling attention in 2:24-26 to the determinative presence of God in the life of man, he indicates that the powerlessness of the wise must have its resolution in the God of the covenant. Man must learn to reckon with Him Who alone can empower men to enjoy life and to live in hope. It is futile for man to labor if his striving does not ultimately receive its benefaction from "the hand of God."

In these verses, the Preacher directs his words pointedly to the covenant sons of Israel, whose abandonment of the covenant at this juncture of her history had become a serious concern. They must be reminded that to depart from their God and His word would avail them nothing. Outside of God all is curse and its consequences. They must carefully consider that while all life is affected at present by the curse (God's burden), God Himself alone is unaltered by it; that although man's life is bound now by the cycle of transitoriness (what Van Den Born styles Rising, Shining, and Passing Away,)[7] God is not so limited; that He truly stands above and sovereignly disposes all that happens to man. They must be made to see that their life and prosperity are inseparable from what God does, whether for curse or for

6. Rousas John Rushdoony, *Revolt Against Maturity*, (Fairfax, Virginia: Thoburn Press, 1977), p. 257.
7. *De Wijsheid van den Prediker.*

blessing. To understand this is to understand whence one's salvation is to be expected. Furthermore, the mention here of the enjoyment of one's labors indicates that the pleasures and activities recorded in 2:1–11 were by no means illegitimate or products of foolish behavior. The Preacher has shown that the real issue is whether or not God is recognized to be at the center of all man's endeavors and enjoyments.

Some have said that the Preacher did not intend to say anything positive about God in these verses, that in conjunction with his pessimism he merely meant to register a complaint about God as if to say that no hope could be found for man in that direction either. Some have asserted that the Preacher's purpose was merely to point up the "arbitrariness" of God so far as the fortunes of men go. Thus, for example, Loader comments that "wisdom has nothing to do with whether a person is fortunate or unfortunate. It all depends on God's unpredictable behavior and totally arbitrary pleasure."[8] This sort of analysis is typical of interpreters who disregard the covenant perspective of the book's author. While it may be true that in these verses the Preacher introduces God in such a way as to imply that all for man depends upon His good pleasure, this is no assertion of God's arbitrariness. Two arguments favor this view. First, in general, to speak of God as "arbitrary" is to accuse Him of injustice and to mock God's covenant word which occurs elsewhere in Scripture, and this the Preacher would certainly have known. Although God's behavior transcends complete human understanding, it cannot be said that it does not possess coherence. That it is impossible always to demonstrate that the ways of God are just does not prove that they are unjust. Second, the text itself presents an important fact: the "sinner" appears there specifically as he who works in vain, and he is contrasted with "the man who pleases Him" (i.e., God), presumably the "righteous" man. Thus the passage can be seen as an affirmation that God's

8. Loader, *Ecclesiastes*, p. 32.

acts are predictably blessings for the righteous, while the statement, "This too is meaningless, a chasing after wind" (v. 26), refers to God's non-arbitrary judgment upon the efforts of the sinner.

In 3:1–15 the Preacher has arrived at the high point of this first segment of his thought. Now that he has introduced God into his discussion he is in a position to explain what the "burden of God" means as it concerns this life. At the same time, his thoughts provide clues to the end of things. In these verses we meet with a rich and complex sequence of reflections that, had we not a broader Scriptural insight, would simply leave us puzzled and bewildered. They are words which covenant-keeping man may read for understanding and encouragement, while covenant-rejecting man in his state of alienation from God is estranged from their meaning.

3:1–8 is, perhaps, one of the most well-known portions of Scripture. At the same time, it is one of the least understood, because we have generally studied the passage out of context and thus have failed to grasp its meaning within the framework of the Preacher's strong emphasis on the God of the covenant that, as we said, came into focus at 2:24. Chapter 3 continues the thought which began there to its forceful conclusion at v. 15. When, therefore, the Preacher exclaims in 3:1, "There is a time for everything, and a season for every activity under heaven," while his intention is to say something important about the life of man, his primary purpose is to emphasize the perspective of the God Who "orders" every single aspect of man's life and actions. He does not here address men with some moral platitudes as to how *they* ought to order their own lives, although frequently that is precisely what he is thought to be doing. The Preacher's concern is not to offer advice to man to teach him how best to behave; he does not prescribe, but describes.[9] The Preacher means that, so far as the life of

9. See, Loader, *Ecclesiastes*, p. 35. "As a rule, the error arises from mistaking these pronouncements for prescriptions."

man is concerned, "God has *His* times and *His* seasons—
there is a proper time for God to do things."[10] There is a
structured order to the life of man, even when it involves
sickness, death, and war; for, in spite of the curse, God does
not permit the world, and man's life in it, to fall into complete chaos. He makes sure there are times for birth, health
and peace as well.

The Preacher has spoken about the God of the covenant
unlike the way the wise men of the nations could speak
about their gods. His words are intended to have a twofold
effect. For the covenant sons of Israel it is essential to realize
that life is not a haphazard affair, that it is not fate or chance
that governs events, but the almighty God Who has, at the
same time, become their God. It is his way of saying that
God is able to keep His word as it concerns them, for He
alone, not man, is in charge of nature and history. Nothing
could indicate more conclusively that Ecclesiastes is not a
book with a stoical fatalism at the core of its outlook. Sec-
ondly, his words here are a direct challenge to secular man
who desires to be god over all things. If pagan man is to
achieve his most basic religious aspiration, his sovereignty
must be able to control time and all that occurs in it. This
has certainly been his ambition. It is the highest form his
idolatry can take, which is why the Preacher attacks precisely at this vital spot.

The "burden of God," the central concept of his book,
would lack force if the Preacher had failed to emphasize
God's undivided dominion over "times and seasons." For all
that pits God in His Kingdom against man in his comes to
its sharpest antithesis at this point. The sovereignty over
time means power and authority over what takes place *in*
time. That is the issue that confronts God with man in his
rebellion. The precise quality of man's rebellion lies in his
supreme aspiration to make nature and history serve and
glorify man. To accomplish that goal he must have the absolute lordship of time and its content. How else could he be

10. Leupold, Ecclesiastes, pp. 82, 81.

his own god? As we mentioned earlier, ancient man certainly had that desire as a chief feature of his wisdom ideals. Rushdoony comments: "In ancient paganism...humanistic man sought to govern time by means of rites whose purpose was to control time and nature. In fertility and chaos cults, men believed that they could make nature fruitful again, wipe out past history and sins, reverse time and order, and regenerate themselves, nature, and history."[11] But we must recognize that modern man has no less a goal in mind. He has only become more sophisticated in his concepts and procedures. Modern man wishes to control all events of time mainly by means of science and politics. By these he thinks he will guarantee to himself security, peace, and prosperity.

This attitude towards time has been constant throughout history. It has proven to be a continuous failure. Perhaps it has been here that man in his rebellion has met with the greatest frustration. Since he cannot reckon with God, he cannot admit God's lordship of time. His disappointment, especially in the modern world, has led him to adopt an alternative attitude towards time. While many still place great faith in man's quest to control time, increasingly many have turned to what they think is the only hope left, to *escape* time. To escape time is to escape responsibility for all one's deeds; it is the nihilistic mind which seeks order through chaos and disorder. But this is equally futile, as the Preacher tauntingly asserts: "What does the worker gain from his toil?" (v.9)

But the Preacher does not leave matters there. He addresses the covenant people with positive words of hope. Reminding them of "the burden of God" (v.10), he directs their thoughts to God's covenant faithfulness—"He has made everything beautiful *in its time.*" (v.11) It is his way of saying that God will ultimately make all things beautiful in time. God can do so because He alone is lord of man's time. It is not their task, then, to be gods over time. They must

11. Rushdoony, *Revolt Against Maturity,* p. 228.

entrust themselves to God instead of attempting to "fathom" God's doings. However, this is no encouragement to idleness and passivity, for the Preacher issues a positive order for what God's people should do *with the time* God gives them. "...there is nothing better for [covenant] men than to be happy and *do good while they live*...[to] eat and drink, and find satisfaction in all his toil—this is the gift of God." (vv. 12f) God calls His people neither to control time nor to escape time, but to use their time "while they live" to do good. The Preacher well knows that the only good God recognizes is that which conforms with His law-word. David had certainly recognized his responsibility in this regard, for he confesses, "My *times are in your hands....*" (Ps. 31:15) In Ps. 34:1 he adds, "I will extol the Lord *at all times....*" Moreover, the good that David would perform was found in God's law, for he declares, "My soul is consumed with longing for your law *at all times.*" (Ps. 119:20) Again, "Blessed are they who maintain justice, who *constantly* [i.e., at all times] do what is right." (Ps. 106:3) It is this injunction that was also on Paul's mind when he wrote, "Be careful, then, how you live—not as unwise but as wise, making the most of every opportunity [i.e., *redeeming the time*]...." (Eph. 5:15) The covenant people are to live responsibly before God. To bolster their confidence in this respect, the Preacher concludes that "everything God does will endure forever." (v. 14) God does not give man sovereignty over time, because God wants men to "revere Him." (v. 14) And we can be certain that the works of righteousness we perform, as well as the deeds of wickedness that men do, will be remembered, for "God will call the past to account." (v. 15) Rushdoony summarizes the matter well: "For the believer, time is God's appointed area for man's opportunity and fulfillment.... The Christian is a pilgrim who refuses to find permanency in time.... In Christ, who is his redeemer, he finds his newness of life and the marching orders for time, so he is fixed as to his faith, and on the march in time."[12]

12. Rushdoony, *Revolt Against Maturity,* pp. 232, 288.

VI

The Moral-Social Order Disturbed
3:16–5:7

In the first section of his book the Preacher had portrayed as broadly as possible the difference between the covenant Solomonic wisdom and the wisdom of the covenant breaker. The fiercest clash in the confrontation between the Kingdom of God and the kingdom of man is bound to be over who controls time and its content, God or man. It involves nothing less than the sovereignty over nature and history. Consequently, it has to do with more than purely personal or individual piety; it concerns the goal of an entire civilizational program. Man in his rebellion against God has fondly placed his hope in self-generated wisdom ideals to build a paradise on earth without God. The Preacher's purpose has been to declare that man's presumed wisdom is "powerless" to succeed against an intractable problem in man and in his world: God has cursed man and his world. As a result there exists a deep-seated "crookedness" that his vaunted wisdom is incapable of straightening out. As long as he refuses to come to grips with the problem of sin at the center of his being man will remain frustrated in his goals. His desire is to be his own god, but there is only one true and living God—the God of the covenant. Unless man learns to reckon with Him, he is doomed to a life of futility and meaninglessness. True wisdom lies in admitting God's lordship over "times and seasons." As God has the power to call men to account, so He alone has the power to make their efforts to build life succeed against the corruption of sin.

From this sweeping generalization over the clash of wisdom ideals the Preacher turns to greater particularity in his treatment of the problems that are necessarily related. Far from ending his discourse on the root of man's problem as it bears on his efforts at civilization, the Preacher considers further the endeavors of man apart from God and what must inevitably be their consequences. In this section he focuses especially on the moral-social *order* that man desires to realize but which, because of the innate crookedness in his being, must inevitably turn out to be disorder. Again, his purpose is to indicate that this result stems from the inherent perversity of human nature and God's curse that is its corollary. All man's aspirations for the perfect community of man are constantly being dashed on the rocks of God's curse which everywhere frustrates his ambitions and projects. His persistent hope for a man-imposed order and a just society only ends in oppression, injustice, and futility. At the end of this section, the Preacher makes clear that only obedient submission to God's word-revelation can provide a foundation for moral and social order.

3:16–22 summarizes the Preacher's initial thoughts on the problem of justice and injustice for mankind's goal of realizing the "city of man." Since the very moment when he succumbed to Satan's word in the matter of the tree of the knowledge of good and evil, man has obdurately maintained that he can know (i.e., decide) all questions of good and evil, right and wrong, justice and injustice. His unceasing attempt to build life and culture apart from God is testimony to his proud obstinacy that his vision of a justly ordered world for man is essentially valid. The Preacher's sole concern is to give the lie to this presumption. 3:16 records his (the covenant-Biblical) verdict on all man's arrogant boasts in this respect: "In the place of judgment—wickedness was there, in the place of justice—wickedness was there." The Preacher does not bother to dilate on the mechanics of the problem. He does not enter into an analysis of social or political order to discuss the best and the worst regimes. He says nothing about the causes of injustice, as to whether or not they arise from social or economic inequality, etc. He merely concludes that wherever one looks "under the sun" there man in his self-declared independence from God cannot realize the perfect (read: "just") society which he confidently expects to attain. Man's efforts at civilization are suffused with injustice as a result of his rebellion, not from time to time, but everywhere and always. In this way the Preacher points to the difference between life *under* God's covenant and life outside of it. His words are not meant to offer solutions to problems where no solution apart from God is possible; instead they address the covenant sons of Israel to encourage them not to depart from the covenant in which lies their only hope.

With the covenant in mind the Preacher in v. 17 acknowledges God's judgment and speaks again of God's control over man's time. This is principally how God's covenant people are to think of the issues of justice and injustice. His words came at a time when Israel was in subjection to the will of the nations, a time when they were the recipients of men's "justice." They must recognize that God appoints times of injustice. At the same time, they must remember that just as God will bring the past to account (v.15) so, too, He will mark a time when He will render judgment on all the deeds of men. It is God, not man, Who stands as the final arbiter of man's acts and accomplishments, and the knowledge that God will judge is the most important thing that God's covenant sons ought to keep in mind.

The Preacher realizes, however, that his listeners require more encouragement than the simple statement that God will judge. They need to understand why God permits times of injustice to thrive. God does this in order to make His just judgment visible. Injustice can only be defeated by justice. Man must be made to see that his way is the way of injustice whereas only God's way is just. Once again, the Preacher means to encourage confidence in the covenant. Accordingly, he declares, "As for men, God tests them so that they

may see that they are like the animals." (v.18) The comparison with the animals has, of course, nothing to do with qualities intrinsic to both man and beast. Nor does the Preacher
mean to imply that God does not regard man more highly
than animals. The testing of men is merely to show them
that they have no advantage over animals who neither build
social orders nor experience justice or injustice. Like the
animal, man is destined to die. It is a fate that "awaits them
both." (v.19) In this respect man's exalted estimation of himself and his ideals are "meaningless." His purposes cannot
withstand the grave and the return to dust.

Yet, although man is like the animal in one important
respect, he differs from the animal in another, no less important, consideration. Many commentators treat the thoughts
expressed in vv. 18–22 as continuous, however, as Leupold
correctly notes, "This verse is not a continuation of the
thought of the preceding verses. They have shown in how
far man and beast are alike. Now there comes a statement
in how far they differ."[1] The Preacher provides a necessary
perspective for the covenant people. Clearly death is not the
end, for after death the spirit of man, unlike the animal,
"ascends to God." The thought is tied once more to the
major emphasis in this group of verses: God will judge both
the righteous and the wicked. This is what is implied in the
spirit returning to God. It is all the more reason, then, that
we should correctly understand the meaning of v. 21. Again,
Leupold has accurately rendered its thought: "There are
not many who take to heart as they ought to the fact that
the spirit of man goeth upward, and that the spirit of the
beast goeth downward to the earth."[2] The covenant people
especially must be reminded that God will bring every activity of man into judgment, for it is the Preacher's way of saying, as Hebrews 9:27, "Just as man is destined to die once,
and after that to face judgment...." From this follows v. 22—
"...there is nothing better for a [covenant] man to do than to

1. Leupold, Ibid, p. 100.
2. Ibid.

enjoy his work...." Specifically, he means their work of "righteousness." It is enough, for man cannot gauge the future. God's judgment need be all that concerns him.

Through a series of reflections in Chapter 4 the Preacher expands on the problems and difficulties necessarily associated with man's claim to build a just social and moral order. In 4:1–3 he draws attention to the fact that the kind of order that man envisions for himself, whenever it is realized in practice, can eventually be seen to split into an irreconcilable dichotomy—the oppressors on the one side and the oppressed on the other. History consistently records that wherever man posits his notions of justice and the good society there the reality inevitably turns out to be a struggle for political power by those strong enough to impose their will on others. The ancient philosophers and thinkers studied this problem with grave concern. From Plato and Aristotle to Polybius and Cicero, books and treatises were written to promote the perfectly ordered and just society. How to solve the problem of tyranny chiefly occupied their attention. Always, it seemed, the strong dominate the weak. Each offered their solution to this problem, but none ever achieved any success in altering the reality of things. In our day we have universally hailed the democratic ideal as the answer to this problem, but all that we have accomplished as a result is the "tyranny of the majority,"[3] perhaps the worst form of oppression yet. Outside the covenant there is no solution to the problem. That is certainly what the Preacher suggests in saying that, so far as humanist man is concerned, the oppressed among them "have no comforter." (v.1) Humanist man has no God Who will judge the deeds of men, consequently no motive to act righteously and to abstain from wickedness. In vv. 2, 3 he makes clear what must be the only outlook on life that humanist man can have when he suffers oppression. His attitude is not one of cynical resignation; he merely reflects soberly on what is

3. C.f. Friedrich A. Hayek, *The Constitution of Liberty,* (Chicago: University of Chicago Press, 1985), pp. 103-117.

inescapable for man in his rebellion against God.

The Preacher's concern is to emphasize that the problem of social order lies in a deep-seated perverseness in the heart of man. It is a problem that cannot be eliminated by his attempts to arrange society according to some ideal blueprint. As long as the evil is *in* man his endeavor to realize the "good life" cannot succeed. According to 4:4–6 that is what he expects to achieve through his labor. The Preacher knows that man was originally created to realize a common cultural goal, one in which all alike would share. However, sin, manifest as envy, succeeds only in ripping his efforts at community apart. "I saw that all labor and all achievement spring from man's envy of his neighbor." (v.4) What is more, man is pertinaciously lazy (v. 5), or he is consumed with discontent (v. 6). All these qualities are meant to stress that man's goal of community without God is bound to fall apart, for nothing can eradicate the crookedness in the nature of man himself.

This perverseness in man, however, need not always assume the exact same characteristics. In 4:7, 8 the Preacher points to another, perhaps an even greater, obstacle in the nature of man that wrecks his attempts at building the community of man: avarice and covetousness. Here he mentions a man who is bent on the accumulation of material riches to the exclusion of all else in order to draw attention to the "loneliness" that seems inescapably to accompany that single-minded pursuit. Always such a man views others as a threat to his store of wealth. Even the members of his family are seen as those who would deprive him of his cherished material gain. He would willingly sacrifice anything, even simple companionship, to guard against its loss. The Preacher knows that God created man for social commerce and interrelationships. God did not intend that man should live alone in the land. In God's program for man wealth was never meant to drive men apart; instead, it should be experienced as a mutual benefit made possible by reciprocity and cooperation. But sin produces in man a covetousness that undermines every endeavor to realize a social order apart from God.

Therefore, with words of exhortation aimed at the covenant sons in particular the Preacher in 4:9-12 emphatically declares that "two are better than one..." and "a cord of three strands is not quickly broken." The advantage of friendship is a feature truly known only to the covenant. Only there can wealth be a factor that does not destroy the community of men, for it is his way of saying that the bonds of the covenant are greater than wealth taken by itself. It is not his purpose to denounce riches, but simply to indicate that apart from God's covenant the covetousness of man inevitably makes all communion between men an impossibility. Inside the covenant man can have but one Master, God, but outside the covenant men have many masters including money.

The Preacher provides one additional reason why man's dream of a moral-social order consistently meets with failure. It is the inconstancy and fickleness of the generations of men who are led to expect benefits from their rulers. When at 4:13 the Preacher declares, "Better a poor but wise youth than an old but foolish king who no longer knows how to take warning," it is not advice that he imparts; rather, he fashions his words as the people themselves would whose loyalties and stabilities change constantly as a result of an altered perception of what would increase their happiness and well-being through the faith they have come to place in a new political ruler. It is a reflection on the hope that people place in political rulers in general and how they are easily disappointed, only to be once again deceivingly led to higher expectations. It is the Preacher's way of saying that political power necessarily turns out to be an unstable good when the people's utopian demand requires more than it can possibly deliver. Each generation longs for a political messiah to usher in paradise. History is not short on demagogues who have repeatedly arisen with attractive new proposals with which to replace a *status quo* that has come to be perceived as regressive and unresponsive. The masses willingly support revolution because they cannot believe that the fault lies in them. The fickleness is evident in that each generation has a different view of the matter, for the Preacher sardonically observes, "There was no end to all the people who were before them. But those who came later were not pleased with the successor." (v.16) Although revolution never achieves its desired result, nevertheless another generation comes along with great faith that at last it will succeed, only to be supplanted by the next, and so on. This is life for man outside the covenant. A deeply rooted problem in man prevents the social ideals of the kingdom of man from realizing a permanent basis.

In 5:1–7 the Preacher advances his argument by responding to his observations on the "meaninglessness" that deeply affects man's life and the inevitable and total failure of any social-moral order that man outside the covenant endeavors to erect. He offers the only solution available; however, instead of addressing man in general, as if there were a common moral prescription available for every man without distinction, he turns with direct admonition to the covenant sons alone. His words are meant to offer them hope and the only firm foundation on which to build the social-moral order. Unless God's own people stand faithfully on the word-revelation that rests at the core of God's covenant with them, the Preacher cannot conceive any possibility for rectifying the innate crookedness of man at the heart of all his difficulties. He does not intend to offer a "political" solution to what is essentially a "religious" problem. Nor does he counsel a studied indifference to the matter, as if God had no regard for the social life of man. It is his way of saying that only in the covenant lies the possibility of a social project for man. If God's own people do not grasp this, how can the world ever be made to see that it is so?

That the Preacher now directs his words specifically to the covenant sons of Israel can be seen from his solemn exhortation concerning the "house of God." "Guard your steps when you go to the house of God." (5:1) The house of God is, without doubt, the temple at Jerusalem. It is clear indication that the Preacher's point of view is solidly Scriptural and that his "wisdom" is not of the general ancient eastern variety. He stands solely on the foundation of the Mosaic ordinances, as is plain from his instructions concerning what is, or is not, to be done in God's house. The law of God is the centerpiece of his educational curriculum.

The temple is a chief part of God's redemptive purpose for His people. It signifies God's presence with His people, for it is the place where He has placed His name and has chosen to dwell in the midst of His people. What is more, it is the principle location where God's people are to bring their worship to the Lord and to commune with their God. That God would dwell with His people is a mark of His favor towards them. Fundamental to God's presence with His people is the word-revelation that is to be found there with Him. It is for this reason, more than any other, that the temple figured so largely in the life of God's people and why the Preacher directs the attention of his listeners to it now. God meant that at the center of His people's lives should stand His word to order their way. We should not be surprised, then, if the Preacher's first injunction at approaching the temple should be one of a keen readiness to hear that word—"Go near to *listen....*" (v.1) All else serves that requirement. How can a man expect to succeed in a world oppressed by meaninglessness and the cycle? It is only when the word of God has priority over all that he does. Man's life must be shaped and directed in every way by that word if he hopes to find a clear path in a world weighed down by sin and the curse. To listen is to obey. To state the matter thus is to specify Who is to have authority over man's life. It is to be God, and God alone.

The Preacher's urgency to make certain that his hearers accord God's word-revelation unquestioned authority in their lives derives from the fact that at this time Israel was being tempted away from the covenant and turning to the heathen world to imbibe its culture and values. It was a period when the Hellenistic culture was spreading rapidly over the ancient Near East, absorbing all in its pathway. The distinctness of the covenant people from the nations was in danger of effacement. At the center of the Preacher's concern stood the question of the final authority over conduct and belief. To a great extent Israel still practiced the forms of godly devotion at the temple, but its attitude there was increasingly taking on the characteristics of heathen customs. This can be seen from the Preacher's staunch warning concerning offering "the sacrifice of fools." It refers to a sort of noisy ostentation before God (quick with the mouth; hasty in the heart) that manifests an unwillingness to submit to His word. Such irreverence displays a self-centeredness that readily imitates the pagan consciousness in its attempt to manipulate its gods for self-serving ends. The Preacher means that, in the covenant, obedience to God must take precedence over everything. Man must come before God to hear and receive, not to demand or explain.

The Preacher has shown that for the truly wise man everything that happens "under the sun" is a legitimate field for investigation. There is, however, one exception—the temple. The temple, as the place of God's word-revelation, may not serve as an object of man's investigation. Rather, there alone man submits in humble obedience. All in man's experience stands under vanity and meaninglessness, but the temple alone is not subjected to meaninglessness. Instead, it alone offers man the only basis for life in a world affected by sin and curse. There man hears God's word and submits to God's lordship over all his life. "God is in heaven and you are on earth." (v. 2) Van Den Born has expressed the idea well: "In the temple is authority and here God establishes your comings and goings. Here God instructs you, and you can only listen reverently. Enter, then, in humility and present your offerings and listen with obedience. Here you do not explain anything, instead everything is explained to you."[4] God has erected His temple and has imparted His word. This is what God has done; if we wish to solve the problem of the social-moral order, once again we must reckon with what God does and take seriously what He commands. The alternative, says the Preacher, is that God will be angry at what you say and destroy the works of your hands (v.6). It can only leave man with the meaning-lessness of "many dreams" and "many words." (v.7) God's word alone is to be taken seriously "Stand in awe of God!" (v.7).

4. *De Wijsheid van den Prediker.*

VII

Man's Heart Controlled by the Power of Want 5:8–6:9

In the previous section the Preacher had focused our attention on the primary causes of man's inability to realize the dream of a perfect social and moral order. While the causes appear varied, in fact every cause is ultimately traceable to a single source—the unremitting crookedness of man's heart. Secular man especially cannot engineer a social project which comports with his ideals of justice and equity, because he lacks a genuine transcendent authority principle solely within his own conscience that is sufficient to offset the centrifugal force inherent in every man obeying the voice of ambition (or, avarice, covetousness, indolence, intemperance, etc.). This dilemma remains unresolvable for man as long as he refuses to heed the voice of God. "When men dream of being god, their only attitude towards all other people and things is to use them to their advantage and profit."[1] This "paradise motive" impedes man's effort to build the society of man and is the chief reason for the oppression that is the inevitable result. The injustices which men are bound to experience cannot be glossed over or palliated by the mere external application of "political" programs. Unless man is willing to come to terms with his sin and God's curse he remains powerless to produce anything but a burdensome tyranny. It is only by turning to the God of the covenant and His word that any hope exists of escap-

1. Rushdoony, *Revolt Against Maturity*, p. 55.

ing this inevitability. But the realization of this truth must begin with God's people, and it must begin at the very center of their communion with God, the temple. There they come "to listen" and to be built up in God's word. In this way alone can they become the "salt of the earth."

This next portion of his book finds the Preacher continuing his probe of man's heart and what unavoidably springs from it. In these verses the accent is altered slightly to draw attention to a unique problem in the nature of fallen man's experience, one that points up a fatal contradiction at the core of that experience. We are to see that man's heart lies in subjection to a power from which escape is impossible. Dictatorial and pertinacious, it is the insatiable power of "want."

The contradiction lies in a transposition that has resulted from man's sin. God originally created man to be in self-control and obedient to God. More than this, man should *have* control of his life; he was meant to possess the power to implement by wisdom and knowledge the Kingdom of God on earth. His chief satisfaction was to be derived from the accomplishment of that end. Because of his rebellion, man has forfeited all powers of accomplishment and has fallen prey to a power which tyrannizes him. His heart has become enslaved to unquenchable "want," a "want" incapable of gratification. Because man did not want to serve God and build His Kingdom, God has given him over to a false want that man can never satisfy. God purposed that man should find perfect satisfaction in His service, but sin leaves man with the illusion of satisfaction that eludes his grasp. Still, the power of want propels man to seek the good things of life, deluded as he is in supposing that the truly good lies in the world and not in God. But if man does not find his ultimate satisfaction in God, as God meant that he should, he stands condemned to serve a master which he can never appease. Augustine's famous epigram, "our hearts are restless until they rest in You [God]", has captured the quintessential problem and has posed the only solution. In this set of verses the Preacher avers just that.

We should be careful to point out that the motive of "want" is not *per se* a product of man's fall, nor does the Preacher suggest this. At the beginning, man was endowed with an "original" want, his chief desire being to pattern his life after God. The problem lies in the redirection of his want from wanting to please and glorify God to wanting to please and glorify himself. The Preacher affirms that the one leads to dominion and productive satisfaction, for body and soul alike, whereas the other can only lead to base servitude, to a ravenous seeking but never ultimately having. However, the Preacher is no moralist. He does not address the problem solely by means of a set of ethical prescriptions. The problem is radical and deep-seated; it requires a major reorientation in man's heart as to what his true want is and what can perfectly satisfy it. Man must come to see that only by reckoning with the God of the covenant can he hope to resolve his difficulty.

The malignant power of want can show poisonous contamination anywhere, but perhaps nowhere with greater harm and misery than in that realm where humanist man especially has placed his highest confidence—in government and state administration. With remarkable insight, the Preacher unmasks the false trust long accorded the political order of man. His diagnosis of the corrupting influence of want is first directed at the government bureaucrat whom men have deludedly believed to be above corruption and the sole guarantor against everyone else's cupidity. We might wonder why in 5:8 he distinctly affirms that a conspiracy among public officials, both administrators and tax collectors, to bilk the people and line their own pockets should provoke little astonishment. We should not be surprised that officers of the government should be capable of such practices. Do not people instinctively expect government officials to be an unselfish and altruistic lot, mere disinterested servants of the public good? Have not men consistently entertained the notion that those who exercise the powers of government are virtuous simply because government as such is viewed as the only instrument of moral rectitude? The Preacher means to expose such confidence for the delusion that it is.

Public servants, because they too are men in whom a profound crookedness resides, are no less corruptible and corrupted by the power of want than anyone else. That they are mere creatures of selfless duty is a conception that must be denied. What is worse, when these men succumb, as they inevitably must, to the insidious power of want the inevitable damaging effect of their actions proves far more extensive than if they had lacked the power of government to exploit, for personal gain, those who are defenseless against them. Naïvely to hope in government as the last bulwark against unrighteousness and injustice is simplistic nonsense, and official corruption should not be cause for amazement. No aspect of man's experience is impervious to the ferocious power of want, no institution exists where it does not penetrate, and when men submit to its insistent demand they will stop at nothing, nor will they be hindered in their consciences, in order to gratify its compelling appetite. Apart from the God of the covenant and submission to His word what can prevent the organs of government from becoming tools of plunder by men who are driven, as all men are, by the keen desire to accumulate the treasures of life? The Preacher cites no other defence.

By means of a series of proverbial reflections, the Preacher, in 5:10-17, succinctly analyzes the problem of man under addiction to want. Quite naturally, "the series begins," declares Whybray, "with that which lies at the root of the problem: the *love* of money...."[2] Money, of course, is customarily seen as the measure of one's wealth. The real concern is with what money can purchase and the perception of its positive benefits for man. However, it would be a mistake to imagine that the Preacher denigrates the value of

2. Whybray, *Ecclesiastes: The New Century Bible Commentary*, p. 99.

wealth. It is not money *as such* that is the root of the problem, it is the *love* of money. The Preacher focuses on the heart of man in its corruption. Money is viewed as a means—in this instance, the chief means—to satisfy the heart of man. Money, along with the wealth it commands, is elevated to a "god-like" status. It is sought for "divine" benefits. It is not for nothing that Jesus asserted that, "You cannot serve both God and Money." (Lk. 16:13) The "love" of wealth means the dedication of one's life to a rival god, a god, moreover, which demands more than a man can possibly give, and which renders to man nothing in return. "Whoever *loves* money *never* has money *enough*; whoever loves wealth is *never satisfied* with his income." To love money, says Jesus, is to hate God. A man besotted by wealth is a man who loves a despotic slavery. Liberty, however, is not poverty, but the love of God.

To be consumed with the desire for wealth is to invite many difficulties. The wealthy, those whose "goods increase" (v.11), are bound to attract unwanted hangers-on to leech and siphon off their wealth. The Preacher is not concerned to specify who they might be; he only points to their expected inevitability. They may be parasitical friends or family, or he may have the ubiquitous tax gatherer in mind.[3] The wealthy only succeed in attracting attention to themselves, a fact of no great comfort to the rich. When this occurs, as it surely must, wealth's benefit becomes less than what it was intended to be, a mere pleasure to gaze upon. If the rich man dares to make use of it he will find himself the object of unsolicited attention.

The life-style of the affluent possesses a disturbing quality which the Preacher also wishes us to notice. Because wealth is everything to the man consumed by the love of it, guarding against its loss or diminution creates a troubled disposition. A surfeit of possessions often proves to be an unhealthy good when no purpose to life exists but that of self-indul-

3. Whybray, Ibid.

gence. The sumptuousness of the rich man's diet is attended by the loss of sound sleep (v. 12). The labor of the ordinary man is less wearisome, in spite of the bodily exertions involved in its performance, than the idle satiety of the wealthy man whose life is one of limitless consumption apart from any work. The point, once again, is not to praise the life of "industrious poverty"[4] by comparing its supposed virtues to that of frivolous leisure. Rather, the purpose is to focus on the sorts of troubles that display themselves when men are given to the exorbitant love of wealth. Instead of rejoicing in a life of productive accomplishments, they stew in an insalubrious anxiety of unregulated luxuriance. When whole societies are caught in the grip of this false ideal of life, as increasingly our contemporary western society seems to be, they are headed for decline.

Those who worship wealth as a god will often find that such a divinity is precarious and fickle. This problem becomes most acute whenever wealth, instead of being received with gratitude and put to responsible and productive use, is simply hoarded (v. 13). Again let us be reminded that the Preacher is not censorious of wealth *per se*; he merely wishes us to see what happens to men who, under slavery to unappeasable want, view wealth as possessing a permanent benefit to its owner. He expressly denies the witless credulity that imagines that wealth can never be affected by, or that it can safeguard against, abrupt changes in circumstances. As he declares, wealth, far from being the unquestioned good which those whose lives are exclusively devoted to its attainment undoubtedly think that it is, can in fact become a positive harm to its possessor, especially when, "through some misfortune" (v. 14), it suddenly and unexpectedly vanishes. To place an inappropriate confidence in the durability of wealth is arrogantly and foolishly to disregard its fragile dependence on unpredictable and uncontrollable events. No matter how wealthy a man

4. Whybray, p. 100.

may become, it is never in his power to guarantee his wealth. The advantages of wealth can be removed. It is the Preacher's way of saying that only in the God of the covenant is there to be found a permanent security for the life of man. On Him alone can men count, for circumstances do not control Him, rather He determines them.

As he has remarked often, as far as this present life is concerned, (humanist) man can truly depend on but one thing: death. Wealth may have some use for men here and now—this he does not dispute—but they cannot derive any benefit from it in the grave. "He takes nothing from his labor that he can carry in his hand." (v.15) It is his way of saying that death is more certain than riches. Too, it is his way of saying that if a man is not rich towards God he is not truly rich. The character of a man's life that is lived in a single-minded pursuit of wealth is debilitating at best. "All his days he eats in *darkness...*" (v.17)—that is to say, in uncertainty. His only response to such unassurance is one of "great frustration, affliction and anger." His obsession does not permit him a moment's peace. Here is the profound self-absorption of the man consumed by merciless want. It is a hard and unrelenting task-master.

As we have by now come to expect, the Preacher, at 5:18–20, once again makes the characteristic shift in his discourse to the covenant and, in particular, to the God of the covenant with Whom man must learn to reckon. For only here may be found the solution to the problem of want in the heart of man. What the Preacher recommends is a strong indication that he does not view the problem as attached to riches *per se*, as if wealth as such were the cause of the problem. It follows that neither does he commend a life of felicitous poverty as the sole conceivable alternative to what, in the minds of some commentators at least, has been thought to be his denunciation of wealth itself. In other words, what man requires is not a renunciation of wealth, along with the energies that are expended in its pursuit, but a heart re-directed from an idolatrous love of wealth to an exclusive love of God. It is in God alone that man can find satisfaction and contentment.Unless riches are accompanied by an enjoyment in them that only God can give, they cannot truly benefit the man who possesses them. "Then I realized that it is good and proper for a man to eat and drink, and to find satisfaction in his toilsome labor under the sun during the few days of his life God has given him—for this is his lot. Moreover, when God gives any man wealth and possessions, and enables him to enjoy them, to accept his lot and be happy in his work—this is a gift of God." (vv.18f)

Man needs to escape the grip of want. Wealth by itself cannot insure such a result. What is more, man has neither the power nor the inclination to realize that goal on his own behalf. He relies entirely on the grace of God ("a gift of God"). However, he is enabled to receive this good when he accepts the covenant totally. A man cannot experience the satisfaction which God provides without at the same time submitting to God's authority over his life as the Preacher had indicated in the previous section, when he spoke of listening to God's word in the temple. In this way he stresses that life in its entirety is God's gift and is unobtainable apart from Him and obedience to His will. It is this thought on which Moses had gravely pondered. In Exodus 33 we read that God's anger burned against His people on account of their persistent rebellion and steadfast refusal to trust Him fully to care for them and to lead them to the land which He had promised to give them. As a consequence, while He would indeed take them to the land that flowed with abundance and plenty He would not journey there *in* their midst. He would not be close to them but would set Himself at a distance. But to Moses the stark horror at the mere thought that God would not dwell in the midst of His people to be near them was enough to elicit from him this heart-wrenching plea: "If your Presence does not go with us, do not send us up from here." (33:15) Moses knew that earthly treasures are of no value to anyone if God be not in them to give man happiness and satisfaction. However bountiful they may appear, if we do not enjoy God in them we can never find them to be a benefit to us. For God alone has the power to make life happy in the time that He allots to man. Nothing in man or in his experience can achieve that end. If we be not rich in God we shall never be truly rich in anything, regardless of our material possessions. The good things of life are only truly good by reason of the goodness of God's presence that must accompany them. When men learn this truth in the covenant they lose the self-absorption that is the distinctive feature of those who are enslaved to want. Such a man, claims the Preacher, "seldom reflects on the days of his life, because God keeps him occupied with gladness of heart." (v.20)

It may seem strange that the Preacher did not conclude his discourse on the bitter problem of want when he had directed our thoughts to the consoling words of the covenant. Why, having shifted the narrative from the earlier negative portion to the positive reconciliation with God and the satisfaction that derives from Him alone, does he return to further reflections on the difficulties associated with man in his crookedness and servility to unmitigated want? The Preacher added observations addressed especially to men who refuse any recognition of the God of the covenant. In particular, his words are aimed at men who mistakenly assume that the real issues of life turn on the question of wealth and poverty, men who fatuously believe that to be wealthy is the highest purpose of life and that poverty represents the greatest of evils. These are men who think that life is good or bad depending on whether or not one possesses material comforts and their attendant rewards, who imagine that the external circumstances of life are all that truly matter. The Preacher exposes this misguided perception for the foolishness that it is. At the same time, his words could not speak with greater relevance for today when whole societies —our own especially—have become ensnared by the single-minded desire to increase their material well-being. When a people's energies are devoted solely to the pursuit of material gain they cannot guess, when things go wrong, that it is God Who frustrates their utopian expectations. It is a bitter experience when God heaps riches upon men and then deprives them of any real enjoyment from them. When we refuse to reckon with Him He may make us choke on abundance.

He continues (6:2), saying that "God gives a man wealth, possessions and honor, so that he lacks nothing his heart desires, but God does not enable him to enjoy them, and a stranger enjoys them instead." There we observe that it is God Who makes men wealthy, and it is God Who enables men to find satisfaction in their wealth. It is possible that God may give the one and withhold the other. All depends on God! It is the Preacher's way of saying that material benefits to man have their transcendent root in the spiritual realm. Were we to chose not to recognize this fact, let us consider that it is possible that the enjoyment of one's wealth may be transferred to someone else. Economics is no autonomous dimension in man's experience. Wealth and its benefit are not inseparable from the moral and religious disposition of the people who seek to reap its advantage.

Apart from God wealth can become a bane rather than a boon. To emphasize this point the Preacher makes a comparison between the long and prosperous life of one who has known only insatiable want and the brief existence of the child who died at birth, whose life therefore never experienced the driving ambition to accumulate material gain. For those who suppose wealth to be the highest good the Preacher counters with the assertion that "a stillborn child is better off than he." (v.3) The Preacher means that the real problem resides in man's heart, for while the man who lived long and enriched himself mightily would seem to be better than one who never possessed so much as an ounce of this world's opulence, still there was less in the latter's experience to drive a wedge between him and God. And if we are not rich towards God we are poorer than we imagine. In the end death overtakes everyone. Of what use is a long and prosperous life, especially when such a life is deprived of satisfaction in the wealth it owns? It cannot guarantee against death, and we recall that earlier the Preacher said that with death comes the judgment.

The Preacher concludes his discussion of man under the power of want, but not without a sharp blow in verses 7–9 at the misplaced confidence of humanist man in his civilizational values and goals. Man is incapable of seeing the irony of his problem. He expends great energy to meet the demands of his bodily appetites, which are the only ones he recognizes to be legitimate, yet he is never satisfied. His labors never cease. They are never enough. For when the Preacher says that "his *appetite* is never satisfied," (v.7) we understand him to mean the *soul* is never satisfied. This is a great dilemma for men who rebel against God. The man who refuses to admit that the material dimensions of his life were meant ultimately to serve spiritual ends cannot fail to be dissatisfied, and eventually disillusioned, with his material abundance, however great. Man cannot find that gratifying his body alone will ever provide the inner stability and self-assurance before God of which he is truly in need in a world that is cursed and subject to death. God alone can satisfy the soul, whether a man possesses much or little. Man must first recognize the poverty of his soul before he can hope to become rich in anything. Those who labor only for the mouth will not find satisfaction, but those who hunger and thirst after righteousness will be filled (Mt.5:6).

Finally, with his characteristic disavowal of traditional wisdom ideals, the Preacher ends by saying that those who pride themselves on their wisdom are no more successful at escaping this dilemma than are those whom they contemptuously disdain as fools (v.8). Man as mere man, whatever else verses 8, 9 might mean, just does not possess the resources in himself to deliver himself from the power of want. To presume otherwise is "meaningless, a chasing after the wind." (v.9)

VIII

The Mystery of Good and Evil
6:10–8:1

To his main theme, that God has laid a heavy burden on man, the Preacher at the beginning of this next section of his discourse, adds the sobering observation that in all man's lot "under the sun" what is crooked or twisted cannot be straightened. God has imposed a curse on man because of sin and man is powerless to remedy his predicament. In obstinate pride man steadfastly refuses to acknowledge God's right; he blindly denies that it is with God Whom, above all, he has to reckon. Man manifests this denial by vainly asserting that he possesses the correct wisdom ideals (civilizational principles) by which to rectify any adversity that comes his way. With naïve presumption he sets out to fashion a perfect world apart from God, refusing to recognize God's imposed burden under which he, nevertheless, must eke out his existence. The Preacher again calls attention to the truth that the covenant Solomonic wisdom unavoidably clashes with the wisdom of humanistic self-sufficiency, for God has His covenant with His people, an altogether unique basis upon which to conceive and construct life. Either men will learn this covenant wisdom and so prosper in hope in a world affected by curse, or they will foolishly reject its sound insight, accepting in its place the sterility and meaninglessness that ultimately attaches to the blandishments of humanism's arguments and goals. No other alternative remains.

The problem addressed in this set of verses is the question

of good and evil, not so much the good and evil that men
do, though that certainly influences the issue, but the good
or the evil that happens *to* man, which seems to come into
his experience adventitiously. In a world impaired on
account of God's curse, nothing in man's experience is reliable and coherent. At different places and times life ran-
domly divides into opposites. Man may experience good or
bad unpredictably. Life constantly changes from some
degree of one to the other. Man experiences wealth or poverty, health or sickness, prosperity or adversity, success or
failure, justice or injustice. All these, and more, happen
sometimes consecutively, sometimes simultaneously in the
societies of men, regardless of what man might presume to
do to control his own situation. Surely much that occurs
may appear to be the result of man's misdeeds or seem to be
attributable to what man in his fallen wisdom designates as
chance, but the Preacher insists that all that happens,
whether for good or for ill, takes place, in the final analysis,
according to God's will. Always what God does determines
the life of man. The centerpiece of this section clearly
underscores this notion: 7:13 states, "Consider what God
has done...."

Previously the Preacher had introduced each segment by
focusing attention on an aspect of the deep problem of
man's life, affected as it is by sin and curse, only to conclude
at or near the end of the section with God and what He
does as that which truly matters. Now, however, the problem
demands that the Preacher not leave God until later but
must acknowledge Him from the outset. He well knows that
the special issue of God's "predestination" is something
which no man will ever accept as a reasoned conclusion; it
must be proclaimed as a premise. Consequently, he
declares, "Whatever exists has already been named, and
what man is has been known; no man can contend with one
who is stronger than he." (6:10) There is no doubt that the
One Who "names" and the One Who "knows" is God,
even as the one who is named and known is man. All that

pertains to what a man is, his character as well as his circumstances, was foreordained in the eternal counsel of God, long before any man either existed or acted. Man's life, the good as well as the bad, must be viewed as the consequence of God's will. The Preacher is saying that man lives ultimately in a personal environment; it is God, not some impersonal nature, that determines the life of man. No greater contrast could be presented to the humanistic wisdom ideals, stretching back into the ancient past, than the Preacher's affirmation that it is the personal God of the covenant, not some mysterious configuration or conjunction of impersonal cosmic forces, Who influences the existence of man and nature.

Recall that in Part I we said that the covenant Solomonic wisdom stood over against the so-called wisdom of Egypt and Mesopotamia, the two most representative covenant-breaking civilizations in the ancient world. The dominant ambition of these civilizations was to explain that whatever transpired in the world, in the life of man especially, stemmed entirely from propitious or inauspicious occurrences of cosmic forces projected as divinities. Such "gods," however, were free to act only in accordance with an ultimately fixed fate. Consequently, it was fate that, in the last analysis, ruled the affairs of men and nature, dispensing its bounty or withholding it strictly in accordance with a capricious destiny. What took place was entirely impersonal and accidental so far as man was concerned. Nothing he might do to take matters in hand could alter things in the slightest. One simply had to accept one's fate. At the same time, men were left free to conduct themselves entirely as they saw fit, for neither good behavior nor evil behavior could influence the circumstances of life.

The Preacher sees this attitude on the part of humanistic man as a contending with God Who is stronger than man (v. 10). Fallen man blames God and complains that God is unjust in what He deals out to men. Sinful man holds that God has no right to order the life of man. Humanistic man is full of "words" (v.11), but his words are only counterproductive. Life appears to be a capricious affair to men outside the covenant who cannot accept that their lives are arranged by God. Such men want desperately to have life under their own control, to be able to divine the future for their own good. But for the covenant-breaker the future is a hidden mystery.

On the other hand, the Preacher's words reassure those within the covenant. For they tell them that their lives are not the product of chance events, but rest in the counsel of God's will. Furthermore, although they do not know what God intends for the future in any specific sense, they nevertheless do know from God's revelation in the temple that the future is Messianic, that God means ultimately to do them good. Consequently, they must not puzzle themselves over the good or the evil that occurs in the world, but must entrust themselves to God Who in the temple has revealed Himself as Jehovah[1] and has given His promise of a certain future that will be governed by His Anointed One. They must not trouble themselves about what life holds nor exercise criticism concerning all that takes place, but instead must practice faith and obedience.

The verses 7:1–6 encourage a definite outlook on life in the light of what the Preacher had just remarked in 6:10–12. He wishes to dispel, especially for those within the covenant, any thought of embracing a life of fatalistic indifference. The truth that God "predestines" the life of man, dispensing both good and evil according to His sovereign good pleasure, is no excuse for the claim that how a man lives and comports himself in the world is of no enduring consequence. On the contrary! The covenant people must understand this preeminently: what men do has eternal repercussions. Some activities indeed are "better than" others. In particular, "A good name is *better than*...," "the day of death is *better than*...," "It is *better* to go to the house of

---

1. Van Den Born, *De Wijsheid van den Predicker.*

mourning *than...*," "Sorrow is *better than...*," "It is *better* to heed a wise man's rebuke *than...,*" etc. By means of a series of contrasts the Preacher makes clear that some things in life hold greater importance than other things. The wise man will choose the better course, the fool will opt for the worse.

Because man cannot contend with God Who is stronger than he, the temptation arises to take life "under the sun" merely as it comes and to regard its pleasures as all that is worthwhile. Because experience seems to teach that it makes no ultimate difference what men do, the fool draws the conclusion that the best that this life has to offer is all that truly matters. His desire is to be released from responsibility and to live for feasting, laughter and excitement. Life possesses no studied purpose and so should not be taken seriously. The next thrill is all that concerns him. Because the fool believes life has no intrinsic purpose, his sole intention is to rollick in the moment. The fool is present-minded, unconcerned for either the past or the future. He is a wastrel and a squanderer of his time, bent only on personal indulgence and self-gratification. He is numb to any notion which says that the fruit of his life will come into judgement at the end of it, therefore, he pays no attention to the day of his death except disappointedly to recognize that it puts an end to his profligacy and debauchery. An entire civilization, when it imbibes this philosophy of life, stands to inherit a neurotic decadence. Nothing else can account for the drug and rock culture of our own day.

The wise man does not forget the seriousness of life. As a result, his days are filled with preparation for death and judgment. He remembers that he must give an account of himself before God. For him a good name means more than perfume, a symbol of life's pleasures. His life is lived to please God and not himself, for "he who seeks for a good name is a person who seeks to do good works in this life."[2] He knows that it makes every difference how men spend

2. Van Den Born, Ibid.

their time during the few days that God grants to them. That is why he more willingly enters the house of mourning instead of feasting, "for death is the destiny of every man," (v.2) and with death the fruits of one's life come into judgement. The Preacher means to encourage the belief that God is pleased with those who are sensitive to the fact that life must be lived in His presence. The future belongs to them; their works will not go unrewarded. Not surprisingly, such a man is quicker to listen to the wise man's rebuke than he is to be lured away by the siren song of fools. (v.5) The wise man in this instance is Solomon, which is to say the covenant Biblical wisdom. In the ultimate sense he is Christ. Men must decide whether his words take precedence over self-interest or not. The choice made will have lasting results.

The verses 7:7–14 are meant to inculcate a certain perspective on the covenant people, especially in the light of God's sovereign control over the good and the evil that happens in the world. In particular, they are not to let the fact of preeminently evil days lead them either to utter discouragement or to the precipitate notion that they must do something to correct the problem. Their course must be to reckon with God and to learn that only in Him can they hope to find a resolution.

It is in the nature of fallen man to want to coerce the circumstances of life. He desires to bend reality to his will. He will employ any means he deems necessary to achieve that result. He will not hesitate to resort to extortion or bribery if these seem to ensure the outcome he wants. It is easy for the righteous to become disturbed by the consequences of this behavior and to respond in kind in order to rectify matters (v.7). But the Preacher warns against being quickly provoked, for such anger is liable to lead to harmful results for the righteous themselves (v.9). It is a great temptation on the part of the righteous to want to right every wrong, to desire to correct injustice everywhere, yet he does not see that his impatience with evil can only turn out to be detrimental to himself. He must be reminded that good days as well as evil days are matters which lie in God's hand.

The folly of his actions, when they have failed in their intended design, leaves the righteous mournfully absorbed in himself and with the present evil circumstances. Instead of accepting life from God's hand and hoping in the future he retreats to a maudlin sentimentality for the past which he mistakenly believes was a better time. The Preacher rebukes such queries as "Why were the old days better than these?" (v.10) It is not the past that the righteous should desire to recall but the future in which they must hope, for, "The end of the matter is better than its beginning, and patience is better than pride." (v.8) The end takes precedence over the beginning because God will bring every deed into judgment. God's people must rest confident that God has a purpose in all He does. Their concern should be not to become distraught at what occurs, but to seek wisdom. Specifically, they must draw near the temple in faithful listening to God's word, for then they will learn that the future is ultimately in their favor. The acquiring of such wisdom has the advantage of preserving its possessor from evil (v.12). The nature of that advantage lies principally in the knowledge of God and His will. They will learn to "consider what God has done", and that no one "can straighten what He has made crooked." (v.13) This is the heart of the Preacher's thought on the problem of good and evil. It is a truth which can only be grasped within the covenant. Apart from the covenant it remains a mystery. God does not permit Himself to become accountable to men. When men learn the wisdom of the covenant, "when times are good" they will "be happy, but when times are bad" they will "consider" that "God has made the one as well as the other." (v.14)

Along with the need to reckon with God's sovereign disposal of man's affairs it is necessary to take seriously the power of sin. From 7:15–8:1 the Preacher considers again that the evil which predominates in all that men do has great strength. It is an especially troubling thought as he,

within the framework of Solomonic wisdom, makes plain at
v. 15. There we observe a striking change in emphasis which
previously attached to the "meaninglessness" that necessarily accompanies the "crookedness" of man's life. Instead of
his forceful comments at humanistic man in his refusal to
reckon with "God's burden" upon his life and world, the
Preacher's words are directed to himself. He begins, "this
meaninglessness life of *mine....*" He had not spoken this way
before; he does so now for a very special reason. The words
may be the Preacher's, but we are to understand that the
person who utters them is Solomon! With the power of sin
the Solomonic wisdom encounters its limitations. Solomon
confesses his powerlessness to deal with sin *at its root.* He is
unable to make either righteousness or wickedness receive
its just deserts. It is the Preacher's acknowledgment that
only God can deal with sin at its core; we must wait on His
Messiah, the true Solomon, if we are to hope for a permanent solution to this inscrutable problem. In the meantime,
God permits wickedness to flourish in order that men, covenant men especially, might come to see that sin is a mighty
agent in the world and its evil consequences cannot be erad-
icated by anything which men might do.

He states: "I have seen both of these: a righteous man
perishing in (i.e., *because of*) his righteousness, and a wicked
man living long in (i.e., *because of*) his wickedness." (v.15)
These words convey the helplessness the Preacher senses as
a faithful disciple of covenant Solomonic wisdom. He knows
that this is not the way life was meant to be, that, in truth,
the reverse should prevail: the righteous should live long
because of his righteousness, and the wicked should perish
because of his wickedness. Clearly something is amiss. Even
the conventional humanistic wisdom ideals have taught this
to be so, as least implicitly. How much more the covenant
viewpoint! The contradiction is profoundly disturbing.

Yet the Preacher is not in despair nor does he counsel
such. Rather, he proceeds to warn the "righteous" against
the attempt to rectify wrongs and evil as if it were in their

power to do so. Thus, at vv. 16, 17 he couples the "overrighteous" with the "overwicked"; for here the term "righteous" is meant to be tongue-in-cheek. The "righteous" are those who, being overly confident of themselves, trust immeasurably in their righteousness as sufficient to solve injustices and malevolent behavior. The Preacher warns that such an attitude and the actions that follow spring from a type of "self-righteousness," which, so far as God is concerned, is a form of wickedness. It is an attitude that seeks to take the place of God in the governance of human affairs; as Leupold comments, "An overstrained righteousness which grows out of conceit and stands ready to challenge God for His failure to reward is plainly under consideration."[3] Such men do not consider the power of sin which is able to resist them and ultimately to recoil upon them. They will experience destruction more certainly than they will accomplish their desired goal. The Preacher advises God's people to grasp this fact and, instead of trusting in themselves, to learn to fear God. Those who fear God will not forget their limitations and run to extremes (v. 18).

Verses 19–22 expand this thought. Most commentators hold v. 19 to be a mere parenthesis, but it is integral to the Preacher's thought. It emphasizes that regardless how valuable wisdom often proves to be, still it will be no guarantee that there is a righteous man on earth who always does what is right and never sins (v. 20). Even the righteous are sometimes at the mercy of the power of sin. The covenant people cannot look to their righteousness, but must look to their God to find assurance against the day of evil. Therefore, they ought not to be quick to condemn the wickedness of others against them when they themselves have not always acted with proper intentions (vv. 20 & 21). Even among the faithful sin can, and often does, gain the upper hand. It is a reminder that the "crookedness" in man is an ever present problem, which he is powerless to solve on his own.

---

3. *Exposition of Ecclesiastes*, p. 164.

A deep sense of the inadequacy of the Solomonic wisdom reappears at v. 23. When he had reflected that good and evil cannot be dispensed by man at his will, that it is foolish to suppose that man of his own accord can straighten what is implacably crooked, the Preacher, as a disciple of Solomon, had wanted to discover exactly how God would eventually bring forth the straight line from the crooked line in this world. We see this when he declares; "All this I tested by wisdom and I said, 'I am determined to be wise'—but this was beyond me'." (v.23) From the viewpoint of Solomon he had recognized that all that comes to pass in the life of man has its final explanation in God's hidden design. But would it be possible to know *how* God intends to remove the presence of evil altogether? Could one discover the way in which God would ensure that good and evil, instead of being inextricably intertwined in the world, would be separated and each receive its just reward? The Preacher knows that the answer to these questions must lie in God. Yet he also wishes to know *how* God will lift the curse with its burden on life and so once again permit life to abound in uninhibited goodness and righteousness. Solomon had no specific answer. From his standpoint the matter appears "far off and profound..." (v.24). He only knows that in the temple God has revealed that He will clarify these matters in the Messianic future.

Still, the Solomonic wisdom is far from useless. Just because the Preacher did not know how in the future God would deal once for all with sin and its consequences, it should not be thought that Solomon's wisdom perspective was devoid of anything salutary. Although he could not find the answer to the ultimate "how" God would act, nevertheless the Preacher certainly knows that the Solomonic wisdom is still necessary for making a true distinction between good and evil, for understanding why men are so prone towards evil, and for recognizing that it is only in the covenant that one can learn the true good and hope in the future perfectly to experience it. Therefore, instead of offering a bitter and deprecating invective against the covenant

Solomonic wisdom, he takes from it what God meant that he should and leaves to God the matter of solving the problem of good and evil. "So I turned my mind to understand, to investigate and to search out wisdom and the scheme of things and to understand the stupidity of wickedness and the madness of folly." (v.25) It is enough that he warn the covenant people against the pitfalls of wicked behavior. Apart from Solomon he could not have discovered "the awesome power of corruption."[4] To learn this is to set the covenant people on the right path.

In his summary the Preacher asserts that though he had searched for the *how* of God's deliverance, "but not finding," (v.28) still not all was in vain. By the Solomonic wisdom he has learned ("discovered," "found," vv. 27, 29) that if evil does exist and has exhibited great power, the fault does not lie with God, but exclusively with man. For, "God made man upright, but men have gone in search of many schemes." (v.29) Wickedness in man's experience is no mere happenstance, no accident of nature, but a deliberately sought-after course of behavior. Man does not practice evil fortuitously; he acts from a mind-set that carefully calculates both its means as well as ends. Sin in man is an active principle, ever seeking more territory to conquer. Far from having a tangential place in his experience, it is the controlling dynamic in all that he does. The Preacher means that sin in man comes to expression as a total philosophy of life and as a civilizational ideal. It is with this in mind that he employs the moral analogy of the seductress—"the woman who is a snare, whose heart is a trap and whose hands are chains." (v.26) Far from denigrating women, he simply uses the example of sexual enticement to characterize the nature of the corrupting power of worldly wisdom. Lust and sexual seduction is a subtle and dangerous temptation to man, when once he has shown a willingness to be enticed by its apparent attractiveness. The temptation to court the

---

4. Van Den Born, Ibid.

humanistic philosophies of life, with which the covenant people seem so often willing to gamble, presents an apt parallel. Were it not for the grace of God (v.26) the blandishments of humanism would have easily succeeded in their allurements, for the power of sin in men, the covenant people included, is such as to leave them defenseless to the scheming wiles of the wicked. Just as a man cannot take a harlot to his embrace without destroying his soul, so too he dare not flirt with humanism's ideals lest he become absorbed in them. For the Preacher it is possible to find "one upright man among a thousand"—a reference to the covenant wisdom and those who live by it—but not "one upright woman," (v.28) for humanism has nothing good in it whatever.

While Solomon may have his limitations so far as understanding what God does and will do, nevertheless he reigns superior to the ideals of life which issue from the covenant-breaker. The Preacher glories in his Biblical Solomonic outlook on life. "Who is like the wise man? Who knows the explanation of things? Wisdom brightens a man's face and changes its hard appearance." (8:1) The covenant people must remain faithful to the covenant. Life has its true explanation here. The hope it induces offers joy, peace, and contentment. Outside the covenant, life is a struggle for goals that cannot be reached, for ideals that cannot be realized, with disappointments that cannot be assuaged.

IX

Man Lives Not by Experience Alone
8:2–9:10

When God first created man, God spoke to him and gave to man an *interpretive principle* by which man was to know himself and the purpose of his life. What God said was meant to be the basis of man's life and culture. Man could not have discovered a purpose for his life had God not expressly communicated it to him. Nothing in man or in his world around him could possibly enlighten him as to the reason for his being or the aim he was meant to realize. God's covenant word, then, was man's original interpretive principle, the basis upon which all his life would have meaning, the foundation that could alone give direction and order to his activities.

In his rebellion against God, man denied that God's word should stand as the interpretive principle for all of life. Still, due to the fact that man was created in the image of God and thus could not escape the characteristics imposed by his nature, he was obliged to adopt some interpretive principle to serve as his authority or cease to be a man altogether. This inescapable demand man understood well; so, at the prompting of the Tempter, he immediately embraced an alternative principle, one totally opposed to the one God had provided for him. Because he rejected God's explanation and ordering of his life, all that truly remained for him was to find these in himself. The result has been that man has elevated sheer *experience* to be the highest principle of interpretation. Rather than to submit his experience to the criteria of God's revelation, man came to assume that his experience was self-interpretive and a sufficient criterion by which to act and to build life. When we trace the outworking of this fundamental supposition in man's, especially Western man's, historical development, we soon discover that his endeavor to live by the ambiguous dictates of experience generates an unresolvable dichotomy. On the one hand, he seeks to follow what to him is a *rationalist* path, which claims that the *logic* of experience is the true voice of authority. On the other hand, he sets an *empirical* course, one which complacently contends that the *fact* of experience should act as the only legitimate master over man's life. Either way, it is experience alone that guides him and determines the course of his behavior.

Replacing God's word with his own experience, man has sought to rely on the consequences of his experience to provide the moral standards for his behavior. He pronounces moralistic judgement, based on what results from his and other men's actions. If the activities engaged in seem to benefit his experience, as he decides what is beneficial, then those acts are necessarily good acts; if, however, the opposite is the case, if his actions seem adversely to effect his experience, if he suffers from his actions in some way, then without a doubt they are morally reprehensible. Here is the sole criterion for every evaluation of good or evil, right or wrong, justice or injustice so far as sinful men are concerned.

Experience stands as the supreme god of humanist man, and by its outcomes he discovers which actions are "righteous" and which are "unrighteous." Because he "knows" with categorical certitude, he is impelled to rectify all actions which his experience sovereignly declares to be bad, for to impede "good" experience is contrary to the will of his god. Such a god would never willingly impose suffering on any man. Consequently, it is man's right to have only good experiences. When they are not forthcoming someone is at fault—specifically, someone *else*, for no man would ever intentionally give himself bad experiences! If he does suffer such experiences, it is intolerable and must immediately be set right. Experience decides that the righteous must be rewarded with good and the wicked with correction and some form of punishment. Divine experience will not endure the contrary.

It is against this background of the secular mindset, with the god-like status that man accords to his experience, that the Preacher continues his discourse on the "burden of God." His words will be devoted almost exclusively to the covenant people and how they should learn to evaluate their own experience in the light of the covenant. They must understand that experience alone is incapable of providing the ethical and religious guidance they require in life. Experience is not sufficient to explain itself, nor may it be viewed as a means by which God communicates his will to them to order their lives. Most especially, it must not be taken as the basis for deciding the outcomes of either righteous or unrighteous behavior. Often righteousness does not receive its just reward in this life, nor does unrighteousness receive the retribution it deserves. The covenant people cannot rely on experience in and of itself to resolve this dilemma, for experience teaches that it makes no difference how men act. God's people must adopt the covenant viewpoint and not trust in their experience. In particular, they must look to the God of the covenant to make sense of their experience. The central thought of this section (8:17) drives home this truth: "then I saw all that God has done." What God does, not what they experience, is all that matters. Man must set his sights not by his experience, whether good or bad, but by the God of the covenant.

In 8:2–9, the Preacher sketches the problem of the oppression of the righteous from the general point of view. That is to say, he explains to the covenant people why they can and should expect wicked men to exercise oppression over others, an oppression which can and frequently does include them, as well as how they as God's people must respond to the problem. This is seen especially at v. 9: "All this I saw, as I applied my mind to everything done under the sun. There is a time when a man lords it over *others* to ("his own"—most translations) *their* hurt." The last part of this verse is mistranslated when it is made to read "his own hurt." It is out of keeping with this context of verses and with the book as a whole. The correct reading is "their hurt," i.e., the hurt of *others*, for we should recognize that the Preacher's concern is with the actions that some men take in order to oppress other men—and, as he means to make clear, the righteous in particular. When we grasp this it facilitates our understanding of the verses 2–8.

The opening verses, vv. 2–6, have usually been held by commentators to mean that the Preacher warns the people not to rebel against some evil *human* monarch, regardless how despotic and arbitrary his behavior may be. However, we cannot accept this interpretation. Instead, we believe that the Preacher is addressing the problem of oppression, that of the righteous especially, within the covenantal framework of the central thesis of his entire book, namely, the burden of God. It is his purpose that the covenant people should understand that the problem of their oppression can have neither its explanation nor its resolution in terms of their experience, but that it must be viewed within the context of what their God does. The "wise in heart" (v.5), i.e., the righteous, will learn to reckon with God in this matter and not to fall into despair at what their experience sometimes turns out to be.

Consequently, in language that God's people alone can be expected to understand, the Preacher, referring to what affects them in this life, introduces God and the covenant at the outset. "Obey the king's command, I say, because you took an oath before God. Do not be in a hurry to leave the king's presence. Do not stand up for a bad cause, for he will do whatever he pleases. Since a king's word is supreme, who can say to him, 'What are you doing?'" (vv.2–4)

The appearance of the word "king" unhappily confuses many commentators, who think it must refer to some human ruler under whose power and authority the Preacher's listeners must presently abide. Why should we assume, however, that the Preacher has some immediate earthly ruler in mind? The thought does not demand it. Besides, the Preacher certainly knew that elsewhere in Scripture God is often referred to as a king. Psalm 10:16—"The Lord is King for ever and ever; the nations will perish from his land." And Psalm 24 closes with repeated references to the "King of glory" (vv.7–10). No one can doubt who is meant. Psalm 93 uses imagery associated with regal splendor and power. There God is "robed in majesty," and His "throne" is established. These and other references support the idea of God as a king. May we not then think that the king in 8:2 is God himself? And if some "earthly" monarch were required, it could easily be Solomon himself, the covenant king, in whom God's wisdom and kingship became manifest on earth. It is certainly within the framework of Solomonic wisdom and authority that the Preacher has been speaking in Ecclesiastes, the total context in which he seeks to impart wisdom to his listeners. Besides, in what sense would God's people, at this juncture of their history, be thought to enter some earthly ruler's "presence" (v.3)? What could the Preacher mean when he says that they should not leave the king's presence? His words make little sense if some human potentate is in mind, but their "covenant" king is a different matter.

The Preacher's words teach that, in spite of the time in which they live, a time when wicked men and civilizations were in the ascendent and the covenant people reduced to a petty and oppressed existence, nevertheless God's people ought not to abandon the covenant. He admonishes them to "obey the king's command," and to remember their oath before God. To depart from the king's presence is apostasy,[1] and to stand for "a bad cause"(v.3) is to adopt humanist man's method for resolving oppression. It is to rely on human wisdom and might. But they must not seek to take

1. Cf. Leupold, p. 185.

the place of God, for God will not become accountable to man; "he will do whatever he pleases." (v.3) Neither does He submit to man's judicial interrogation. No one may say to Him, "What are you doing?" (v.4) Plainly, what transpires in the lives of God's people to a very great extent lies concealed in His sovereign determination. That He does not always disclose His reasons is not cause to take matters into their own hand, nor to turn from the path of covenant faithfulness. In time God will resolve the problem of the oppression of His righteous ones. The "wise heart," instead of rebellion or unfaithfulness, will consider that God is sovereign over time and history, therefore over what they experience. They will "know" that God has His "proper time and procedure for every matter." (vv.4,5) The Preacher reminds us of what he had said in 3:1–15. The covenant people must not allow the present circumstances of "man's misery," i.e., the misery caused by man, to discourage them. Even though it "weighs heavily," God is capable of acting on their behalf. He is Lord of their time.

The wicked, as by now we have come to expect, refuse to reckon with God's sovereignty over man's time (vv. 7 & 8). They steadfastly believe that they are the captains of their souls, the masters of their fate. But the Preacher, in order to bolster confidence in the covenant, reminds them that man possesses no power to decide the future and to control events, thus to triumph everlastingly in his wickedness. God can and will ensure that their evil will recoil upon them (v.8).

It is one thing when oppression is experienced under those outside the covenant, it is another thing when it seems to reside at the heart of the covenant itself. Sometimes the righteous are suppressed even within the "church." In 8:10–13 the Preacher observes that what constitutes the inheritance of the righteous is usurped by the wicked. The ungodly take control of the institutions of the covenant and receive the honors due the righteous. "Then too, I saw the wicked (buried—some translations) *draw near....*" (v.10) At the same time, "those who used to come and go (i.e., the righteous)

from the holy place and receive praise in the city *are forgot-
ten....*" The "holy place" refers to the temple and the "city"
is the city of God where His presence is located. Both sym-
bolize the Kingdom of God. These are the inheritance of
the godly; but wicked men have taken over and exercise
control. The church in history has repeatedly become apos-
tate. The Preacher can at least indicate why this happens—
it has to do with a lack of discipline in doctrine and practice.
"When the sentence for a crime is not quickly carried out,
the hearts of the people are filled with schemes to do
wrong." (v.11) Nevertheless, the righteous can comfort
themselves that God will not permit such ungodliness in His
Kingdom long to triumph. Indeed, the Preacher can say
that, "Although a wicked man commits a hundred crimes
and still lives a long time, I know that it will go better with
God-fearing men, who are reverent before God. Yet
because the wicked do not fear God, it will not go well with
them, and their days will not lengthen like a shadow." (vv.
12, 13)

The overall thought in this group of verses is that, based
on experience alone, the covenant people cannot discover
what the fruits of their labors will be. Instead, from the
standpoint of experience, one may quite often expect that
"on earth...righteous men...get what the wicked deserve,
and wicked men...get what the righteous deserve." (v.14)
What is essential for the covenant people to know, and what
their experience will not make known to them, is that this
contradiction has its explanation in "all that God has done."
(v.17) More than this it is impossible to discover. "No one
can comprehend what goes on under the sun. Despite all his
efforts to search it out...." (v.17) Why God permits the labors
of the righteous and the unrighteous to reap inappropriate
rewards is not given to them to know. But their chief concern "on earth" should not be their experience. A faithful
adherence to God and His word should dominate their
attention. However, the Preacher does not mean that they
should devote themselves to duty for duty's sake, as if they

could expect no reward for their righteous behavior whatever. He affirms the opposite: "So I commend the enjoyment of life, because nothing is better for a man under the sun than to eat and drink and be glad. Then joy will accompany him in his work all the days of the life God had given him under the sun." (v.15) The Preacher means that God can cause the righteous to prosper contrary to the appearance of their experience. Nevertheless, patience and hope must take precedence over experience, whether good or bad. One is reminded of Paul's words in Romans 8:24, 25; "For in this hope we were saved. But hope that is seen is no hope at all. Who hopes for what he already has? But if we hope for what we do not yet have, we wait for it patiently."

In 9:1–10, the Preacher sums up his thought on the problem of what man experiences in the world, why the experience of the righteous does not accord with their righteousness, and why the experience of the unrighteous does not correspond to their unrighteousness. He urges the covenant people not to test either the validity or the usefulness of the covenant solely by their experience. They should focus their attention on God, not on themselves; then, they will conclude as the Preacher does that "the righteous and the wise and what they do are in God's hand...." (v.1) If they rely wholly on interpreting their experience, they lose the one valid basis for distinguishing themselves from the ungodly. To confirm this thought the Preacher observes that "All share a common destiny." (v.2) No man, righteous or unrighteous, escapes death. It is the "fate" that "overtakes all." (v.3) If death is the consummation of man's experience, then what value can be placed on what men experience? The criterion by which the covenant people are to live their lives must be something other than their experience. For men outside the covenant experience is the law of their existence. To them everything depends on experience. But for the covenant people any attempt to live by experience must result in bitter disappointment and cause them, of all men, to be most miserable.

But having warned God's people not to put confidence in their experience, the Preacher places a positive message before his audience. He encourages them to stand firm in the covenant, for that is their one great hope. "Anyone who is *among the living* has hope—even a live dog is better off than a dead lion!" (v.4) With the words, "among the living," the Preacher has much more in mind than mere physical existence. For to be "among the living" means to be "in the covenant." It is they who are truly alive! It does not matter what their experience may be as long as they remain in the covenant. When he claims that a "live dog is better off than a dead lion" the Preacher means that the worst experience of the righteous is better than the life of the wicked, though they triumph like lions. "For," he continues, "the living (i.e., those in the covenant) know that they will die, but the dead know nothing...." (v.5) This refers not just to death as such, but to the judgment death brings with it. It is the judgment of God that will set matters right for the righteous and bring retribution on the wicked. This is what the righteous "know." This is what the "dead" (i.e., the covenant breakers) do not consider. For the ungodly, there is "no further reward." All that they can expect to gain is in this life only. Everything with them will vanish with death and they will never again "have a part in anything that happens under the sun." (v.6) The implication is not so for the righteous! They have a "further reward." Their experience in this life is not all that matters. What they love (righteousness) and what they hate (unrighteousness) will be remembered. The promise to them is that, in spite of death, they will have a part again in all that happens under the sun.

How, then, ought the righteous to live? The Preacher answers in vv. 7–10. They are to go about their business with gladness and "a joyful heart." (v.7) They should take thought that God has them in mind—"it is now that God favors what you do." (v.7) They are to live their lives under God and in recognition that what they do is not in vain. Life now should be taken seriously, as the context in which to store up treasure for the reward that will ultimately be theirs. Consequently, the Preacher commands, "Whatever your hand finds to do, do it with all your might...." (v.10) God's people should serve Him and His Kingdom with no half-hearted effort. It is in life that they should labor for everlasting fruit. In death, all opportunity in this regard vanishes, "for in the grave, where you are going, there is neither working nor planning nor knowledge nor wisdom." (v.10) That is, there is no achievement of these things then. Death is the end of the covenant people's opportunity to work for any further reward. Let not experience be the guide, but let faith in God and in His reward be the basis of covenant life.

X

Life's Consequences Not Subject to Man's Control 9:11–11:8

By now it seems the Preacher's incessant harping on the central theme of his work—the burden of God—has begun to reverberate in the mind like a persistent and unremitting refrain. The burden of God is, in the first place, the curse of God on man's sinfulness and "crookedness," the chief reason for the failure and frustration that persistently spoils every effort of his to realize the ideals of the kingdom of man. The Preacher stands on the firm foundation of the Solomonic wisdom, the covenant Biblical wisdom as a whole. He does not hesitate to assault the self-declared autonomy of man from God, for he knows full well that man will have to reckon with God if he hopes to find a solution to the problem of the "meaninglessness" that overshadows his life and endeavors. Time and again, he has shown us that only in the covenant can the burden of God be transformed from curse into blessing, for it is not the burden of God as such that must be lifted from man's world, but the burden as curse. Man must recognize that because of his own "crookedness," no deliverance can be hoped for from man. He looks in vain to his civilizational ideals, which in truth are aspiration for self-deliverance. Life and genuine culture can only be found in the covenant.

Yet the Preacher has often stressed that those within the covenant may not always expect immediate relief from the pressure of God's burden. They may sometimes have to undergo more arduous trials than do those who stand apart from the covenant and refuse to acknowledge God's acts. The Preacher reminds us that God has His purpose, therefore His people should not take their sufferings as excuse to depart from the covenant and adopt the ideals and lifestyles of the nations. Rather, all the more firmly must they adhere in faith to its glorious promise. The Messianic future belongs to them; God will not forget them. Though uncertainties and disappointments may come their way, God, Who is God of "times and seasons," has the power to set matters straight for His people. They must not permit despair to control their outlook; they should labor with joy and hope, knowing that God favors what they do.

The Preacher has not finished his declaration of the futility that dogs man's life. In his final lament he stresses that life's consequences are not subject to man's control. Man may possess splendid gifts and abilities to build up life, but he cannot guarantee that he will be able to use them. He may find himself at the mercy of events and occurrences that can nullify his talents. Man's accomplishments are not in strict accord with the means he possesses within himself. In this way the Preacher extends his thought, begun in the last section, that man ought not to look to his experience in order to gauge the success or failure of his labors in this life. Time and chance stand back of all man's work and govern his life without his being able to control them. Nevertheless, while man's life is not in his control, it is in God's control, for "time and chance" are at His disposal. Once again the Preacher will make plain that this lesson can only be learned in the covenant after he has reflected on man's powerlessness to be god over his life and thus to ensure that events will turn out as he plans and anticipates.

Beginning at 9:11, the Preacher draws our attention to a variety of factors and incidents that demonstrate that for man's life in general, there can be no guarantee that the means man is able to employ toward his goals can ever achieve them. "Time and chance" (v.11) can easily overrule the activities of man. Thus, the fastest runners do not always

win the race, though that is what we would, under most circumstances, expect to happen. But that is precisely his
point! Circumstances cannot always be depended upon. A
runner sprains his leg. One slower by nature and less well
trained wins the race. Similarly, the strongest men in com-
bat do not always prevail. Reasons may vary; it does not
matter. What is normally the case is not invariably so. Neither can the intellectually gifted count on becoming wealthy,
even though we might suppose that they especially would
have the knowledge to achieve riches. A man of surpassing
skills is not guaranteed success. Man may not place his confidence in the gifts and talents which are his. And, as the
Preacher has often reminded us, death is the most important factor of all. Quite suddenly it may overtake man, without warning; "no man knows when his hour will come: As
fish are caught in a cruel net, or birds are taken in a snare,
so men are trapped by evil times that fall unexpectedly upon
them." (v. 12) Should this occur, man's greatest talents cannot avail.

A man may possess outstanding capacities, yet because of
circumstances in which he happens to be born or that sur-
round his existence, his unique gifts lie unrecognized and
unused. In vv. 13–16, the Preacher provides one example of
such unmerited neglect, the calamitous consequence of failure to recognize genius. In a besieged city every acknowl-
edged means has been exhausted in the effort to turn back
the enemy. However, intones the Preacher, there was one
man in that city who could have and would have delivered
that city by his wisdom, but he was not consulted. The one,
magnificent talent that he possessed could not be employed
for the simple, yet astonishing, reason that he happened to
be a *poor* man. Because he lived in poverty, he was over-
looked by the rich and mighty, those who had responsibility
for the management of public affairs. Perhaps the people's
social prejudices would cause them to look disdainfully on
this man and so to disregard his special wisdom. His social
and economic standing prevented his gifts from being used.

And so "the poor man's wisdom is despised...his words not heeded." (v.16) This city was captured and great destruction followed, all because "time and chance" governed in the circumstances.

The rule of "time and chance" over human affairs excites a rational repugnance, not merely because it negates a person's special talent and renders it otiose, but, more distressingly, because it controverts generally the rule of righteous wisdom in human social experience. Wisdom—that developed insight and understanding so needful for the building up of life—is improvidently neglected, while in its stead there flourishes the vexatious and short-sighted predilection of the fool, with the unavoidable result that the lives of all are at the mercy of his folly and suffer from his conduct. From 9:17 to the end of chapter 10, the Preacher reflects proverbially on the various ways that foolishness, when once it has seized the helm of life and society, can destroy the work of wisdom and cause life to advance on the pathway of instability and precariousness. It is a disturbing truth that people will often prefer the rule of the fool to that of the wise, despite the fact that the fool's behavior only produces ruination and loss. History presents the clear record of the fool's success and man's singular unwillingness to heed the counsel of true wisdom. The foolhardiness of the ungodly steadfastly undermines the effort of wisdom to be heard.

The contrast between wisdom and foolishness is, as stated in Chapter I, a chief concern of the "wisdom literature" of Scripture. The Preacher mentions it here to show what a considerable difference it makes when men choose the one or the other. At 9:17, 18 he briefly indicates how difficult it is for wisdom to be heard, as well as how easy it is for foolishness to offset it. "Time and chance" would seem to render wisdom weak and foolishness strong. "Wisdom is better than weapons of war, but *one* sinner destroys much good." (v.18) But the Preacher knows that the issue rests in the difference between God's righteous covenant and the behavior of sinful man. It is necessary to make plain to man that apart from God's covenant man does not build life, he can only destroy it. The problem is the crookedness in man, for, says the Preacher (10:2), it resides in his "heart." Because the heart of the fool is bent in the wrong direction he is incapable of performing any real good. The simplest matters readily reveal just how incorrigible he is. "Even as he walks along the road, the fool lacks sense and shows everyone how stupid he is." (v.3) Wisdom is acquired at great expense (a reference to the "perfume" of v.1) but stupidity comes easy and requires little effort to defeat the good that wisdom seeks: "a little folly outweighs wisdom and honor." (v.1) Wisdom is constantly being robbed and made of no effect by the counter-actions of the fool. God gave man wisdom to make life prosperous and productive, but sinful man knows only how to pervert God's good gift.

If we glance at our own culture and society, we can readily understand what the Preacher means. The folly of those who have assumed positions of leadership clearly reveals just how difficult it is to persuade people that the policies of socialism and welfarism are destructive of the health and lasting prosperity of the economy and society as a whole. Wisdom can demonstrate the virtue of free markets and capitalistic enterprise, yet people's moral blindness will quickly lead them to believe in statist visions and goals without ever considering the burdens and costs they impose. Moreover, people will more easily succumb to arguments promoting the supposed beneficence of statist education, because of its specious free cost, than recognize that what has emerged is an oppressive system designed to foster ignorance and guarantee incompetence. When sinners gain control of the social program, we may expect that foolish consequences will inevitably follow.

The Preacher has observed that there are times when the fool is awarded the honors and privileges that rightly belong to the wise, and the wise the deserts of the fool. It is a glaring contradiction, but not one to cause surprise, for such a reversal stems from the power of foolishness itself. Men are full of "error", in this instance "the sort of error that arises from a ruler." (v.5) It is a critical reflection upon humanistic man's ideals of government and society, for the mention of "rulers," in both verses 4 and 5, can to refer to "the powers that be" in any sense in which man's way is established. Under such circumstances, men willingly exalt the fool and, at the same time, reduce the "rich" and "princes" (the "wise" and "honorable") to insignificance. It would seem that nothing could prevent such things from happening. However, as always, the Preacher encourages neither despair nor escapism. "If a ruler's anger rises against you, do not leave your post; calmness can lay great errors to rest." (v.4) The Preacher recognizes that events can turn against the righteous; indeed, they can expect reversals. But they should not for any reason leave the covenant; rather, they should continue to work "calmly" towards its restoration. They should do nothing hastily or precipitately, but, in a mood of tranquil confidence, await "time and chance" to turn in their favor. Messiah's time will come.

Life is full of unexpected changes. Through a series of examples (vv. 8–11) the Preacher reminds us of how men may be affected by unpredictable events. Man is easily frustrated in his labors. The outcomes of life do not rest in man's hand.

Not surprisingly, the wise man and the fool learn very different lessons from this fact. Whereas the wise man counsels prudent advice, the fool's words are full of folly and wicked madness (vv. 12, 13). The fool refuses to reckon with "time and chance" and so "multiplies words" (v.14) to no avail. In truth, he cannot reckon with God. His wickedness knows no bounds to the pretense of his own divinity. The righteous do not wear themselves out as does the fool, whose lack of discernment is evident even in the most mundane matters (v.15).

It is a good thing when a circumspect magistrate is in charge of governing the land. Even though in himself he is wicked, by God's grace he may nevertheless exercise

authority with discipline and responsibility. He may genu-
inely act in the capacity of a servant, his advisors as well
(v.16), and so benefit those who dwell under his jurisdiction.
When a prince governs with self-restraint and for the good
of his people, the land can enjoy peace, harmony, and prosperity. But it may not always be so! The ruler in the land
may be lazy (v.18), or he may be given to luxurious and riot-
ous living (v.19). He comes to believe that "money is the
answer for everything." (v.19) Such are the principles of the
fool. Governments run by such men cause everyone to suffer from their injustices, for they will use their powers to
extract from people what they would not otherwise be willing to give. Taxes can become an intolerable burden when
sinners are in command. However, warns the Preacher, the
righteous ought not to rebel even in their thoughts, for that
is to court the disaster of fools whose only wish is to foment
revolution and chaos. Such behavior is, once again, a refusal
to reckon with "time and chance" and may prove to be
harmful to those who act so recklessly.

Finally, the Preacher, having revealed his knowledge of
what "time and chance" mean for man's life, turns with positive words of exhortation to the covenant sons of Israel.
Although he has addressed them throughout this section, he
now directly exhorts them as to how to behave, subjected as
they are to uncontrollable events. They must lift their hearts
and minds to the God of time and chance; they must rise to
the level of faith in His promise. Instead of permitting
inscrutable turns of events to dominate their thinking, they
should put their hands to the task with full expectation that
their labors shall not ultimately be in vain in the Lord. The
verses 11:1–8 encourage the covenant people joyously to
labor on behalf of God's Kingdom, despite what the
Preacher previously had said about the apparent capricious-
ness of time and chance. Here also the Preacher makes the
final transition in his thoughts that leads to the resounding
conclusion of his book. The "logic" of the burden of God is
nearing its end as far as the covenant Solomonic wisdom is

concerned.

"Cast your bread upon the waters, for after many days you will find it again. Give portions to seven, yes to eight, for you do not know what disaster may come upon the land." (vv.1,2) Here are words intended to enjoin the covenant people to begin, and to proceed, in the only way available to them—namely, "in faith." Many interpretations have been offered of this well-known passage in Ecclesiastes. Most likely, it is an analogy drawn from the risk-taking involved in the sea commerce of the day.[1] The casting of bread upon the waters probably refers to the financial investment that is hazarded in overseas trade and shipping. It would certainly have required courage and faith to take the risk, for both life and property were placed in great jeopardy. Such journeys constantly subjected commercial traders to the perils of storms and marauding pirates. One stood to lose all that one possessed. On the other hand, if the enterprise was successful, wealth and treasure would most definitely be the return on one's investment. The stakes were indeed high. The point is, if nothing is ever ventured then nothing is ever gained. However, the Preacher does not mean to suggest that it is just a roll of the dice, a gamble and nothing more. He is certain that the covenant people can count on eventual success, because God will guarantee it. But they must learn that it is not readily granted. Through faith and patience their labor will reap its reward. It is the Preacher's way of saying "the righteous shall live by faith." (Ro. 1:17) Although experience says all is useless, faith says every good work shall produce its fruit.[2] Two emphases stand out in these thoughts, as Leupold comments: "The emphasis lies upon the certainty of reward as well as upon the fact that this certain reward will not be received at once."[3] It will be "after many days," that is, in the future, the days of Messiah's reign. Even so, faith should not be blind faith. Hence,

1. C.f. Whybray, p.159; Loader, p.126.
2. Van Den Born, Ibid.
3. Leupold, p. 256.

says the Preacher in v.2, spread the risk around so that if some things should fail others will not. Although the righteous labor in faith, time and chance continue to operate over man. Only now they are viewed in the proper light as "the work of God, the Maker of all things." (v.5) Although we may not have complete comprehension of that work, we may rest assured that it does not fail. And in the temple God has revealed that He works to bring in the Messianic future.

Much in this life appears to be either inevitable or random.[4] "If clouds are full of water, they pour rain upon the earth. Whether a tree falls to the south or to the north, in the place where it falls, there will it lie." (v.3) But this should not cause God's people unbearable concern. Nor should they allow themselves to be distracted from the job of sowing and harvesting God's Kingdom. They may not sit idly by, supinely awaiting the arrival of perfect conditions[5] before they decide to act. It is vain and irresponsible to look for propitious times in order to build God's Kingdom. At all times, good or bad, His people should be found diligently in His service. Do not squander time and opportunity by endeavoring to penetrate the veil of secrecy surrounding God's work in the realm of "time and chance!" (v.5) His promise and covenant are sufficient. Therefore, let every moment, "morning" and "evening" (v.6), find the covenant people assiduously at their tasks. It is not for them to know how matters will turn out. The obligations of the covenant may not be made dependent upon what we experience now. Instead, take hold of life joyously as the time to work on God's behalf. Remember that days of "darkness" lie ahead when no work shall be possible (vv. 7, 8), nor fruits stored up for everlasting life.

4. Whybray, p. 159.
5. Ibid.

XI

The Solution of the Matter
11:9–12:14

In his final words (11:9–12:14) the Preacher presents the solution to the great problem of man's crookedness and God's curse, as far as it is to be understood within the framework of the covenant Solomonic wisdom. The Solomonic wisdom—the Biblical wisdom—provides the only perspective upon which God's people can and must rely. It has been the Preacher's purpose to make them see that they can depend upon nothing else. Under the pressure of God's burden the words of secular and humanist men are worthless, but when the covenant sons of Israel listen with faithful obedience to God's word-revelation in the temple they can hope to find the answer to its inexorable power. There they learn to reckon with what God does and to take seriously all that He commands. It is there, too, that they discover that God has promised a future to those who remain faithful to His covenant. That future belongs to His Messiah. When he comes, the great weight of God's burden will be lifted from man's world, for through him the crookedness and sinfulness of man will be removed. In the meantime, God's people must not let the present misery and dislocation of their experience in the world cause them to become disconsolate. Knowing that the future is theirs, they must work with gladness and unwavering purpose.

The Preacher instructs his listeners to "accept life!" (11:19) Although life and the labors of men—their works of righteousness in particular—often seem to be robbed of their fruits, God's people must not be deterred: "Be happy, young man, while you are young, and let your heart give you joy in the days of your youth. Follow the ways of your heart and whatever your eyes see...." (v.9) The Preacher addresses especially those who are young and in the strength of their years, those for whom life and everything it has to offer still lies before them to be taken in hand for the achievement of productive goals. It is that time when we set our purposes and choose on which pathway we will tread. It is in youth that we select the purposes for our labors and choose the path for their accomplishment with eager anticipation. Go and do, says the Preacher! Hold nothing back! Do not trouble yourselves over "the cycle!" The world belongs to God, and He has granted you the opportunity to build up life. Give yourself to life in all its richness and fullness. If things seem to be perverse and distorted, do not let that bother you. Rather, while you have strength in your limbs and ambition in your souls, put your talents and gifts to work. Life may not turn out as you expect, but you must not permit its uncertainties and disturbances to impair your energies.

The work which the Preacher encourages is not merely activity for activity's sake; he incites youth to labor on behalf of the Kingdom of God, to expend their efforts for its increase in the world. Their endeavors must be defined by what God wants, not simply in terms of what pleases them. Immediately upon prompting them to accept life with diligence and enthusiasm, he sternly reminds them that all that they do will have its ultimate consequence in the light of God's judgment: "...but know that for all these things God will bring you to judgment." (v.9) Here the Preacher reaches the summit of his thought. At the beginning, he proclaimed the heavy burden of God as the theme he intended to expound. Now he uncovers its fullest significance. With his emphasis on God's judgment, the Preacher brings to light what, as a disciple of Solomonic wisdom, he has all along been determined to make clear—that in all man's experience under the sun, God is to have undivided priority. His people must be fully convinced of this truth and willing to live in unhesitating compliance with its demand. They, of all people, should act and work with the certainty of God's judgment as the mainspring of motivation. They must recognize that what God *will do* He *is* doing unto completion. Then they will reckon above all else with what God does, seriously *now*, while they possess the vigor of youth, not *later* when the possibilities for building life have been greatly diminished by old age. The covenant must predispose how God's people think and act and look at life from the outset. Their lives are not theirs to do with as they please, but are to be used for works of obedience in all that they do and wherever the ways of their heart may take them.

Because the Preacher has contrasted the joy of the days of youth with the "pleasureless" (12:1) years of old age and inevitable death, some commentators have concluded that death is his most urgent concern. For example, Loader maintains that in this text of verses and throughout his book death is "the only certainty there is for the Preacher."[1] This is to misunderstand his thought. The most certain thing in the Preacher's view is not death, but God's judgment. Indeed, the stress on death is meant to set in bold relief the greater certainty of God's judgment, for death itself has no meaning for the Preacher outside the context of the burden of God. Since the Preacher's intent has been to make clear the priority of God over man, all that comes within man's experience, including death, must be viewed as subservient to that purpose. As a faithful disciple of Biblical Solomonic wisdom he could not think of the matter otherwise. It is not death itself that matters, it is what death involves: the judgment of God on man's life. The latter should occupy our attention with sober reflection more than the former; however, only within the covenant will men ever truly learn this to be so.

1. Loader, p. 131.

Youth, the years of bodily strength and mental alertness, is the time to work not just for temporal rewards but for everlasting fruit. It is not the time to wile away one's life in a vain pursuit of bodily enticements and trifling and dissipating gaiety. On the other hand to fret about what the future holds is an enervating disease. Youth is a great time in life, but it can also be a dangerous time, since the appetites of the body are keen and can promote an inordinate absorption in the temporal satisfactions which this present life offers. Such preoccupations tempt one to follow after strictly worldly interests with a vain disregard for God's judgment. Hence, the Preacher warns the covenant people that "youth and vigor are meaningless" (v.10), these qualities of life possess nothing permanent in and of themselves. They are destined to perish. If during their time we do not use them for godly purposes, we shall truly have wasted our opportunity to produce lasting results. So, "banish anxiety from your heart and cast off the troubles of your body." (v.10) Self absorption is not in keeping with covenant responsibility.

Instead, "Remember your Creator in the days of your youth, before the days of trouble come and the years approach when you will say, 'I find no pleasure in them'." (12:1) Replace self-concern with God-concern at the center of your life. Do not wait until later to do so, but do it now, in the days of your youth. However, do not foolishly believe that youth can deliver one from the burden of God's curse. The Preacher is talking solely about the opportunities available at that period in a person's life. Secular man looks to youth as a time to feed irresponsibly on life's pleasures. For the covenant youth it is the time to remember their Maker and to live life in His covenant, the only guarantee against the onslaught of the curse.

By emphasizing God as the Creator, the Preacher draws attention to the whole realm of creation as the field of man's endeavor. This is especially so for those within the covenant. The entire creation provides the territory in which to work on behalf of God's Kingdom. But also, by mentioning the word *Creator*, the Preacher has made it plain that man lives in God's world and that God will take account of what man does there. As Van Den Born comments, "Everything that the world as God's creation has to offer may be accepted, but not in order simply to consume it upon yourself, rather in order to make a contribution according to God's law."[2] Moreover, "God the Creator will investigate everything that has occurred, because man has lived in His world and has eaten and has drunk of His wealth, and has had the enjoyments of His gifts."[3] Consequently, "Blessed is the man who considers in these splendid, bright days that he lives in God's world, that he eats and drinks of God's riches. He will remember his Creator and work to honor Him...before the dark days break in and man must abandon his work."[4] The man who furnishes works of obedience will assuredly have a share in the future Messianic age. Youth is the time to be obedient to God's covenant.

In 11:2–7 the Preacher, by means of a series of metaphors, paints a portrait of life when old age sets in, and when eventually death takes over. At last "the dust returns to the ground it came from, and the spirit returns to God who gave it." (v.7) This return is, as pointed out earlier, an allusion to the judgment to follow. It is when "man goes to his eternal home..." (v.5), when man goes to his destined reward. The covenant people are to understand that in the judgment God rewards His people as well as condemns eternally the wicked. Youth is the time to consider this and to work towards that appointed destiny. When the Preacher says, "Remember him," (v.6) he means, do not let the days of opportunity slip by.

From 12:8 the Preacher concludes his thoughts on man's problem and God's burden. It is often referred to as the "epilogue," just as 1:1–12 has been called the "prologue." It is also that portion of his book that has given modern inter-

2. Van Den Born, Ibid.
3. Van Den Born, Ibid.
4. Van Den Born, Ibid.

preters their greatest difficulty, for, with few exceptions, commentators strongly influenced by modern textual-critical methods of Biblical study have confidently concluded that the verses 12:8 to 12:14 cannot possibly constitute the original ending of the book of Ecclesiastes. These cannot be the Preacher's own words, but must be those of a later editor or editors. Whybray asserts, "It is universally agreed that this final section of the book is the work not of Qoheleth but of one or more persons who were familiar either with the book in its present form or at least with its contents...the epilogue is the work of an editor or editors who gave the work its present shape."[5] Loader maintains that the "epilogue is obviously not the work of the Preacher."[6] This viewpoint is also held by Delitzsch, among others.

We are compelled to ask, what is the evidence to support such a hypothesis? As for "external" evidence, there is none. The argument is strictly on the basis of "internal" evidence, the supposition that a distinct change of mood, one more positive sounding, has suddenly emerged after a long and relentlessly negative and pessimistic message has failed to show a way out of man's overwhelming dilemma. In our view, this notion is entertained not as a result of the failure of the Preacher to sound a positive note throughout his book, which we have repeatedly demonstrated to the contrary, but because of the failure of interpreters theologically and covenantally to grasp the thought content of the book. Because interpreters view the book as not unlike humanistic wisdom in general, they speculatively assert that some later "redactor-disciple" felt obliged somehow to salvage the book for the Jewish community, which would have had difficulty in accepting the book devoid as it seems to be of any mention of the "torah" or law as the way to reap certain blessing and prosperity. No Jew would have believed that God's commandments were not the correct prescription for life. Therefore, the argument concludes, the utter negativ-

5. Whybray, p. 169.
6. Whybray, p.133.

ism had to be softened so as to show that the Preacher did
not mean either to denounce or to declare useless law-keep-
ing in Israel.

We need not waste much space responding to this
hypothesis. If we do not begin with the covenant, so far as
the book is concerned, we shall not end with it either. We
have offered an interpretation which throughout takes this
view into account. It may be unacceptable to the modern,
critical mind, but we suggest there is no other way to
explain the book as belonging to the canon of Scripture. We
believe that it does belong there and that the "epilogue" fits
perfectly as the concluding remarks of the Preacher himself.

When in v. 8 the Preacher declares, "Meaningless! Meaningless! Everything is meaningless!" he repeats at the end
what he had said at 1:2. At the start he announced the curse
as man's central problem. He does so again at the conclusion to remind his listeners of what is in store for man outside the covenant. It is a warning to them not to abandon
the covenant which is their only hope in a world crushed by
the burden of God on man's sin. This is what they may
surely expect to inherit if they depart from God's solution
for man's problem.

12:9–12 contrasts sharply, and is meant to contrast
sharply, with what the Preacher had reiterated in v. 8. Here
he returns once more to the covenant. Because he speaks in
the third person, commentators have felt justified in maintaining that these verses were added by another. But when
the Preacher speaks this way it is to direct attention to the
basis of covenant life in God's world. In vv. 9 and 10 the
word "Preacher" or "Teacher" refers to Solomon and the
Biblical Solomonic wisdom in general. It is the Preacher's
own claim to speak from that standpoint, to insist that his
words are God's words and do not derive simply from his
own insight. Solomon was supremely the wise man for Old
Testament saints. But when the Preacher adds that "the
words of the wise are...given by one Shepherd." (v. 11) he
refers to God as the real source of those words. It is his affir-

mation that God's covenant word is the only foundation on which the covenant people must base their lives in a world profoundly disturbed by man's corruption and God's curse. He adds emphasis by immediately warning them that nothing further may be added to that word. (v.12) One is reminded of Rev. 22:18 where the same warning was given at the end of the New Testament canon. It is a good reason to believe that the book of Ecclesiastes may be the conclusion to the Old Testament canon. The words of wisdom that God's people are to live by must be no more and no less than what God says. Anything besides is not only of no value but positively harmful. That is why he adds, "Of making many books there is no end, and much study wearies the body." (v.12) Not that the Preacher is an anti-intellect and therefore views books and learning as a waste of time, nor does he insist that we need our Bibles and nothing more. It is that man's learning and study has nothing to offer if they are not grounded in God's covenant word. Humanist man exhausts himself in an endless search for truth and knowledge, which has as its sole achievement the contradiction and undermining of God's word. But God's word alone shall stand (Isa. 40:8). The infallible Word is the only locus of certitude in a world caught in the grip of the cycle. How important it is that God's own people especially understand this!

"Now all has been heard," (v.13) exclaims the Preacher. What is meant to be known has been clearly stated and nothing essential remains to be said. The covenant, with God's sovereign Word at its center, is that alone upon which God's people can expect to be firmly planted in hope for the future. They stand in need of nothing besides. God has graciously revealed to them all they require for guidance and authority.

And so, the Preacher, despite the "meaninglessness" that pervades all of life and its endeavors, counsels neither despair nor escapism as the answer to its devastating burden. He does not pronounce life useless and unworthy of any governing ideals whatever! Quite the contrary! The covenant people are to assume the responsibilities of the covenant and to labor on behalf of its propagation and enlargement in the world. They have a purpose to life; it is to "fear God and keep his commandments, for this is the whole duty of man." (v.13) This should not be taken as mere concession in the face of utter hopelessness, but as a confident belief that, although man cannot do anything to rectify his situation, God can. What is more, these words contain marching orders not simply for individuals but for a total civilizational endeavor, for they pertain not to a portion of man's labor but "the whole duty." God will bring all man's work into judgment. Man's work does not go for naught, but, whether it is good or evil, will receive the reward it justly deserves. With his concluding remarks, we are once again reminded of John's closing comment in Revelation which aptly describes the final division between those who remain faithful to the covenant and those who refuse its gospel: "Blessed are those who wash their robes, that they may have the right to the tree of life and may go through the gates into the city. Outside are the dogs, those who practice magic arts, the sexually immoral, the murderers, the idolaters and everyone who loves and practices falsehood." (Rev. 22:14f)

Conclusion

Ecclesiastes, when properly understood in the light of Scripture, has an unambiguous and timely message. If the interpretation that is presented in this study does not accurately represent the thought of the book, it is difficult to comprehend how it should be viewed as belonging to the canon of Scripture. In what alternative sense could the book be seen to conform to the message of Scripture as a whole, a message which undeniably conveys God's covenant of redemption as the only hope for fallen man? This is not to claim to have exhausted the book's meaning. Doubtless there are insights which we have neglected. But, surely, the book must reflect the same basic viewpoint of the whole of Scripture if it is to justify acceptance as a part of its corpus.

We think the viewpoint of Ecclesiastes is apparent: man must relinquish his self-declared independence from God his Creator and Redeemer if he does not want to have lived his life truly in vain. God and His word must have undisputed sway over all that man does "under the sun," and true wisdom, knowledge and understanding, which are so inescapably necessary for the life-building activity of man, are dependent upon a faithful adherence to His authority and promise. Ecclesiastes arrives at this perspective primarily by the *via negativa*; that is, it drives home what must be the inevitable consequence for man *apart from* the covenant. When the Preacher announces, "Meaningless! Meaningless! All is meaningless!" he declares what a life must be that refuses to

reckon with God and to take seriously what His word commands. Man's would-be autonomous wisdom is of no value
for anything. If man would be truly wise, let him see that
true wisdom begins with turning to God and to His covenant as the only foundation upon which life in this world
can be built.

The words of Ecclesiastes address the problem of man on
a civilizational level. They speak to men as kingdom build-
ers of one sort or another, as workers either on behalf of
God's Kingdom or man's kingdom. Each kingdom perspective is founded on a philosophy of life, on a word of wisdom
that clarifies both the starting-point and the goal to be
achieved. Man in his rebellion has proudly looked to self-
generated wisdom ideals to erect paradise on earth. He
confidently believes himself to be in possession of the correct
agenda for life and culture. He steadfastly denies that his
civilizational endeavors must conform to what God says. It
is the purpose of Ecclesiastes to expose as false the self-sufficiency of humanist man's ideals. In particular, it means to
disabuse God's own people of the pretentious claims of secular man and to encourage them to remain faithful to the
only wisdom viewpoint in which they can hope to succeed.

It is tragic that many Christians in our own day have
found that living in obedience solely to God's word, while
useful perhaps for personal and subjective interests, is quite
unacceptable for the total program of culture. Across the
spectrum of the Christian community a growing acceptance
of the humanistic wisdom can be disturbingly observed.
Nowhere is this more apparent than in precisely those institutions where knowledge and understanding are particu-
larly sought after and transmitted. In how many schools and
colleges have the blandishments of humanistic wisdom
ideals met with nearly decisive success? The agenda of secular man, the vision of life that issues from his philosophy of
man and culture, having usurped the substance of the educational process, have left to Christian truth and understanding only the appearance of presence, and that rapidly

fading. Is the Christian community in the academic world abandoning the covenant viewpoint? In every area of learning, whether it be politics, economics, sociology, psychology, or literature, the ideals of fallen man have acquired great awareness and respectability.

The Preacher's own time was much the same. God's people were being led astray by the siren song of Greek and Hellenistic cultural ideals, and their faith in the covenant was being eroded. Called of God to minister to this growing apostasy, the Preacher came forward with the wisdom of God's covenant word. But that word was delivered with a powerful reminder that God's people cannot depart from the covenant without paying a heavy price. Outside stands God's curse. To adopt the humanistic wisdom is to inherit its negative consequences. If the message of Ecclesiastes seems to echo so pessimistic a note, it is in order that God's own people may know what is at stake.